CW00500015

A CAGED MIND

HOW SPIRITUAL UNDERSTANDING CHANGED A LIFE

MARIA ILIFFE- WOOD

Foreword by

DICKEN BETTINGER ED.D

IW Press

First Published in Great Britain by IW Press Ltd 2022

The front cover artwork is used with permission from Michelle Mackie

Cover graphic design: 18 Design Ltd

A catalogue record of this book is available from the British Library.

ISBN-13: 978-1-8383330-5-8 (Paperback)

ISBN-13: 978-1-8383330-6-5 (e-book)

IW Press Ltd, 62-64 Market Street, Ashby de la Zouch, LE65 1AN

www.iliffe-wood.co.uk

For Mum
with love and gratitude
for doing a great job
when you had such difficult material to work with

And for Ash
who showed me the cage door was open

PRAISE FOR A CAGED MIND

Between 2013-2019 sales of self-help books were up by 12%, running somewhere around 18.6 million volumes. People of all walks of life buy self-help books. They read one book after another hoping to ease their discontent and unhappiness. Maria Iliffe-Wood's book A Caged Mind is part of a new genre of self-help writing, that takes the reader through the writer's own personal experiences, as a way to show the healing journey. I was captivated as I read A Caged Mind. I was drawn in by the author's willingness to reveal herself on the page. I found myself relating to her stories and anxiously turning the pages to see what and how she negotiated the next experience. The writing is true and honest, as Iliffe-Wood takes us on a journey with her through myriad twists and turns of her life and what she saw and learned as she went. And like any great book, as I read A Caged Mind, I was both entertained and educated. This is a must-read for anyone who is a human. The last self-help book you will ever need to read.

— JULES SWALES, WRITING TEACHER AND POET

A Caged Mind speaks straight to the heart and soul. I was mesmerized from the first line to the last. In simple, skillful language that crafts vivid images of moments in her life, the author describes spiritual insights that freed her from limits she created with the power of Thought. Through Maria Iliffe-Wood's unvarnished voice and generous sharing, we see what became possible for her outside of the caged mind. Her story is the human story, our story, and can awaken in all of us hope, freedom from suffering, and astonished awareness of a daring, creative, full way to live. I will recommend this book to all of my clients at home and abroad. To quote the last line of the book, "it is good!"

LINDA SANDEL PETTIT, ED.D. SELF-EXPRESSION COACH AND INTUITIVE SPIRITUALITY TEACHER, 3 PRINCIPLES PRACTITIONER, AUTHOR, COUNSELING PSYCHOLOGIST, RETIRED, OWNER, 3 PRINCIPLES INTERVENTION, LLC

Maria's journey to freedom from the cage of her thinking is brutally and beautifully intimate....heartbreakingly real and inspiring!

— STEVE CHANDLER, AUTHOR OF CREATOR AND RIGHT NOW

A Caged Mind is a beautifully crafted compilation of stories and insights that are deeply personal, but also universally human. You will recognize yourself -- and all of life --throughout this book. I can't recommend it enough!

— AMY JOHNSON PH.D, AUTHOR OF JUST A THOUGHT: A NO-WILLPOWER APPROACH TO OVERCOME SELF-DOUBT AND MAKE PEACE WITH YOUR MIND AND THE LITTLE BOOK OF BIG CHANGE: THE NO-WILLPOWER APPROACH TO BREAKING ANY HABIT

A Caged Mind is full of simple yet powerful vignettes that caused me to stop and reflect. Maria's story resonates because it could be any of us with a head full of insecurities, trapped within our own cage. Who hasn't experienced the torment of feeling unloved? Maria's exquisite writing brings each scene to life. Each detail is felt. Each emotion lived. Delicious prose had me catch my breath, like "stood in a pure wool camel coat that hid a multitude of sins." I love Maria's analogy of the caged mind and how we innocently imprison ourselves within that cage. In this wonderful book Maria shines a light on where the cage ends and infinite potential abounds. If you're looking for hope, look between the lines in this book and see what resonates with you. Maria shows us that the catch to the cage is in the quiet of our own minds.

— JB HOLLOWS MSC FRSA, AUTHOR, SOCIAL ENTREPRENEUR, MOTIVATIONAL SPEAKER.

A Caged Mind is a beautifully touching, inspiring book. Written with vulnerability, honesty, humour and clarity, Maria talks about her own journey in a way that gently encourages us to reflect on our own experience of life from a deeper understanding of the mind and inspires us to examine more deeply the truth of who we really are. For those of us willing to look in this direction, this book is timely and truly transformational.

— STEF CYBICHOWSKI, INTERNATIONAL TRAINER, SPEAKER AND TRANSFORMATIVE COACH

CONTENTS

FOREWORD

The human mind
cannot imagine
its own infinite potential.

We all have personal stories. Our stories can be entertaining, boring, inspiring, off-putting, or profound. But it is the storyteller that can transform a personal story into a universal teaching story, a story that shares insights that inspire your own insights.

Maria Iliffe-Wood has shared her story in such a way that her insights have the potential to guide you to insights that will do for you what they have done for her. Maria's insights helped her to realize that she is far more than she thought. As a matter of fact, her true self, like your true self, is ever present beneath her personal thoughts, feelings, experiences and even her body. A glimpse of this truth set her free from the imagined limitations and judgments of her own thinking that she believed to be true! She became free of the caged prison that had seemed so real to her. It allowed her to embrace with understanding and compassion all of her shortcomings and to celebrate with gratitude all of her gifts. This happened to her, and the good news is, this can happen to you!

Storytelling is one of the oldest arts among humans. It has long been recognized as a powerful way to pass along lessons learned to others in the community. Its power is that it can by-pass the intellect and touch people in their very souls. It awakens our capacity to transcend, or as Maria says, to transmute our limited mind view. Listen to Maria's skillful and rich storytelling with an openness and innocence, and you too may feel something stirring and shifting inside of your being that lifts your spirits and guides you to a more loving and understanding life. Realising this new understanding for yourself will not only help you, but will help create a healthier world!

Maria is a friend, fellow student, colleague, wife of my good friend Ash Wood, writer, fun, insecure, insightful, flawed, strong, kind...yes, and yes, and yes...but she is so much more! Her true self includes all of this, but within her essential core is a vast, wise, aware, creative, loving spiritual being. Maria got a glimpse of this through progressively revealing insights that have transformed her life. Reflect deeply on Maria's story, and see what the intelligence behind life, your wisdom, has in store for you. I hope that some day soon you will be sharing your love, your compassion, and your story of transformation with others!

Dr. Dicken Bettinger Ed.D
Licensed Psychologist (Retired)
Author: Coming Home, Uncovering the Foundations of Psychological Well-Being

INTRODUCTION

We won't know
what a life means
until it's over.

I didn't set out to write this book. I enjoy writing for the sake of writing and I do so most mornings. I met my soon to be mentor, Jules Swales in 2017, who introduced me to Jack Grapes Method Writing (JGMW). Soon after I joined her class and practiced the JGMW, writing every day. Before long it became apparent there was a theme to my writing. When I flicked through the pages I noticed a number of stories and realised this could be the beginning of a new book. That is the power of freedom from a caged mind. You can't even imagine what wonderful things life has in store for you.

The stories are grouped into several sections. Each section depicts aspects of my steps to freedom. Not that there are any steps. It is not a process to follow. The stories are not in chronological order. The process is more like a 'join the dots' game, where the picture emerges and you have no idea what the picture is until you reach a certain point in the game.

Whilst it was an understanding of Three Principles that changed my life, I am not attempting to explain them, (apart from the brief introduction which comes next). This book attempts to show the impact of the Principles on me and to point you in a certain direction. The rest is up to you.

My fervent wish is that as you read these stories, you might recognise aspects of yourself in the pages and see that you, too, can break free from your own caged mind.

With much love

Maria

THREE PRINCIPLES - AN INTRODUCTION

The Three Principles were introduced to the world by Sydney Banks. He had a remarkable experience that changed his life, during which he realised a simple but profound understanding about how the mind operates. He knew that this would make a huge difference to humanity. It certainly made a difference to me.

Sydney Banks set out Three Principles that are true for each of us. When we get an indication of how these Principles work, we can use our minds to give us a more enjoyable experience of life.

This is not a dictionary definition of the Principles, so if the words don't land well with you, see if you can find words that suit you better.

THE PRINCIPLE OF MIND

There is a divine intelligence that works through all of us that does not come from the brain. It's what brings the body into existence, keeps the heart pumping, the lungs breathing and cells regenerating. It's what gives us life and is the source of everything. Sydney Banks called it Mind. It is universal, constant and unchangeable. Mind acts as our guide throughout life, even when we are not aware of it. Like gravity, Mind always does its job in the background; most of the time we don't pay it any attention.

THE PRINCIPLE OF THOUGHT

We are thinking beings. Aware of it or not, consciously or subconsciously, we think all the time. It is through the power of Thought we experience life.

Thought is the tool we use to create our experience. Everything is brought to life through the power of Thought. It is the lens through which we view our reality.

The power of Thought is more like an energy than a language. It creates all of our mental activity. Babies have the power of Thought creating mental activity, and therefore their experience, long before they have a language to explain the content of thoughts.

Thought is neutral in its own right. It's what we do with Thought that determines how we experience life and it's through the power of Thought that our experience can change if we choose.

THE PRINCIPLE OF CONSCIOUSNESS

It is through the Principle of Consciousness that we, as human beings are able to observe life, to be aware of life and to be able to experience Thought. Without Consciousness we would have no experience of life.

Consciousness is endless and boundless. Our thoughts arise within Consciousness. In this well of Consciousness lie all the answers we seek. It is an inner wisdom, a quiet knowing, an innate intelligence. When we remember it is there, we can look to that innate intelligence to guide us.

NOT THREE PRINCIPLES BUT ONE

Whilst Sydney Banks talked about three Principles, he was keen to point out they are all one. If you grasp only one of the Principles, you already perceive the trinity. The three are inseparable.

FREEDOM

Being introduced to the Principles was the most profound thing that ever happened to me. It changed my perspective from the inside even though nothing on the 'outside' had changed. I shifted from an existence mired in fear and low self-esteem to a life filled with ease and joy and a greater sense of wellbeing.

We all yearn for freedom in our lives, not recognising that it is freedom from our own thought-created reality that is the answer. The Principles guide us to find this freedom. As Sydney Banks said often, 'We are only one thought away from a nicer experience of life.' Thought is the 'missing link' Sydney Banks refers to, in all his books.

If you would like to find out more about the Principles I have listed, some of my favourite resources at the end of this book.

PROLOGUE

I wanted someone to love me,
not realising that someone
was me.

I lived in a caged mind. Like a fish is oblivious to the water, I was not aware of the cage.

My life was enviable. I owned a beautiful, modern home, a sports car. I bought designer clothes. I had many friends, enjoyed a wide and varied social life, and travelled the world for both business and pleasure. I ran a successful company and most blessed of all, I had a wonderful marriage.

I felt I didn't deserve a jot of it, and I ran scared that one day I would do something stupid; I'd get caught out and everything would come crashing down around my ears. This created a level of anxiety that ran like a fault line through my life. I was in a perpetual state of angst, waiting for the plates to shift and my existence to go down the toilet.

I wanted to feel better, happier, more confident, peaceful, and resilient. I wanted to feel more than, or at least equal to, rather than less than everyone else. I didn't know how, but I knew it was a possibility, albeit one that stayed beyond my grasp.

A self-development nut, I attended countless courses, read hundreds of self-help books. I became overwhelmed by it all and spent months in therapy. For years I kept a therapeutic journal. I don't want to total up the thousands of pounds I spent in an effort to learn how to feel okay and good enough, to feel the way everyone else felt, or so I thought. There had to be something wrong with my thinking, so I looked for the 'right' way to manage my thoughts in the hope that someday I would feel worthy.

Nothing made a difference. Until I came across an understanding that changed every-thing. All it took was one 'aha.'

I had been looking for something outside of me that would fix the inside of me, until I discovered that the answer had been within me all along.

These simple principles were all it took for me to experience my life in a whole different way. "Whole" being the key word. I realised my wholeness. I wasn't broken and I didn't need to be fixed. There was nothing to change. The cage disappeared. It was an illusion, a limitation I had created unconsciously.

When I reflect on my life before I came across the Three Principles, I notice how tiny the cage was, and how it had restricted my existence. I thought I was ambitious, but believe me, I had no idea of the extent of my own potential.

Since then, my life has blossomed in ways I had never dreamed possible. I have an energy and a zest for living, and a freedom beyond anything I could have imagined.

I didn't realise what I searched for was freedom from my own thought patterns. The self-doubt, judgement, and criticism that existed in my mind did not have to be believed. The door to the cage was wide open. All it took was for me to see it, and I was free.

PART I

A CAGED LIFE

In the confines of my mind
I wither. Outside are dreams
I dare not imagine.

My life was a caged existence. Limitations, beliefs, and assumptions prevented me from living a full and happy life. They constrained and bound me.

I lived with a background noise of fear, timid thinking, and a feeling of never quite being good enough. I knew I carried a load of baggage from my childhood, but after years of self-development and therapy, I was none the wiser about how to live without it.

I was a prisoner of my own thoughts, and the stories in this section show how this manifested in my life.

1
THE SCALES OF GIVE AND TAKE

A fever had knocked me for six and I was laid up in bed with an off the scale temperature and lead-filled limbs. I'd been ill for a few days and ploughed on regardless, until it got the better of me. The doctor said an ambulance would take hours, and as I lived on my own, he'd suggested I ask someone to take me to Accident and Emergency. My boyfriend, Trayton, was the logical choice.

I'd had my eye on Trayton for a long time before we'd hooked up. He was a looker, that one. A skilled dancer, loads of women wanted to partner up with him. I was lucky he'd chosen me. I had an idea that he'd be kind and generous, that he'd be a caring person who would look after me as much as I would look after him.

He had turned to me when he was at a low ebb and I'd dropped everything to take care of him. I'd helped him through what he called his 'great depression.' I'd been there for him when he needed me. I picked up the phone and explained the situation.

"Will you take me to the hospital?" I asked. I lay in bed with a winter duvet and a weighted blanket heavy on my body. Despite the grey flannel pyjamas, a baby pink fleece and purple thermal socks, I had a layer of sweat on my skin and still I shivered. My mouth was like the Sahara Desert, my head felt like the inside of a blacksmith's forge. The noise in my temples was an incessant pummel of a kick drum by an inebriated demon. My eyes were closed to shut out the white light of the phone in my hand.

My long, ash-blonde hair was matted and sprawled over the pillow, a discarded pack of Paracemetol caught in the strands. The clock on the side table said 7:30 pm.

"I can't," he said. "I've just ordered take-away for me and my brother." Where was I in his pecking order? (A thought I would not have until much later.) "Okay," I said. "No problem."

The ambulance arrived at four in the morning. The paramedic asked me some questions, but I couldn't get my tongue around the answers. Later, I was told I'd made no sense. I was taken to Leicester Royal Hospital with a severe kidney infection and wasn't discharged until a few days later. Trayton didn't visit me because he had to work. He didn't pick me up to bring me home because he was too busy. He didn't come to look after me while I recuperated. He had things to do. Yeah, of course I was disappointed, but I'm a big girl.

I was gutted when the relationship ended, but there came a point when I looked back and saw how the scales were lopsided. The balance of give and take was way out of kilter.

This relationship helped me to learn that beauty needs to be more than skin deep. What I wanted was a partner, someone who would care for me as much as I cared for him. Someone willing to put my needs above his from time to time. A man who would love me as much as I loved him.

2

NOLITE HOMINUM

Be optimistic
Be positive
Be happy
Be generous to others
Be careful of other people's feelings
Be agreeable

Be bright
Be intelligent
Be confident

But be quiet

Be encouraging
Be trusting and trustworthy

Be a ray of sunshine

Stay on cloud nine
Stay on top of things

Stay on it, no matter what

Do well
Work hard
Try your best at all times
Never let up

Don't be sad
Don't be miserable
Don't gripe
Don't rant and rave
Don't swear
Most of all don't swear

Don't protest
Don't remonstrate
Don't lament
Don't make a fuss

Take it on the chin
Grin and bear it
Take it lying down

Don't be human

3
WHO'S COUNTING?

After a long chat with Jules, my friend and writing coach, she said she had to go as she had to finish some editing for a dear friend. Hours later, it dawned on me that she was talking about me. At no time had it ever occurred to me that I could be counted as such because I don't count myself that way.

On the abacus of life, I don't count.

Go back to where you came from," Saint Peter will say when I stand at the Pearly Gates. "You're useless. You're good for nothing, a piece of shit. You don't count." Perhaps he won't say shit, but something like that. "What did you ever do?" He'll ask, "to earn your place in Heaven?"

> Don't tell me about all those people you helped.
> That doesn't count.
> Don't tell me about all those hands you've held.
> That doesn't count.

Don't tell me about all the tears you've watched
and waited to dissolve, the woes you've listened to,
the brows you've soothed.
They don't count.

Don't tell me about all the good deeds you've done,
the hours you've given,
the sacrifices you've made.
They don't count.

Don't tell me about all the people you've befriended.
The sick people you've cared for.
The loans you've made
with no expectation of payback.
They don't count.

Don't tell me about the books you've written.
The awards you've won.
The testimonials you've earned.
They don't count.

Don't tell me about all the leaders
whose lives you have helped to transform,
the relationships you have helped to heal,
the conflicts you have helped to resolve.
They don't count.

Don't tell me about the kindnesses to strangers,
the donations to charity, the volunteer hours,
the causes you've championed.
They don't count.

Don't tell me what a good partner,
good parent, good sibling,
good relative you've been.
None of that counts, either.

Nothing counts.
I don't count.

But who's counting?

4

MY ESCAPE

Living in a small terraced house with a family of eight was like living in the baboon enclosure at the local zoo. When the noise didn't overwhelm me, it was the fear that got me. I was scared the whole time. Scared of the sharp edge of my mother's tongue, the thwack of a wooden spoon on the back of my leg, the searing heat of a leather belt scorching my backside. Fear kept me bowing to my mother's every demand, kept me at the twin tub for hours with laundry piled on the floor by my feet, kept me at the kitchen sink or doing household chores, when all I wanted to do was have some fun. Fear prevented me from making friends or being part of the in crowd. It kept me on the outside of life. My escape was a captivating book.

I would sit for hours on end in a little wooden chair in the corner of the bedroom, my right thumb in my mouth, lost in a book. I read every chance I got. At the bus stop, on the bus, in the school playground and on every car journey, no matter that I would get carsick. I wanted to lose myself in somebody else's life. I would hide from the chaos and the fear. I would read other people's stories, real or imagined, taken away from my angst-ridden life to other, more beautiful, exotic places. Immersed in a book, I ceased to exist. I could forget I was the odd one out, forget I could never measure up, that I was nothing.

The best times were when I had the bedroom to myself. I remember on one occasion I'd run upstairs, grabbed a book off the shelf, sat down and dropped it into my lap. Anne Frank stared up at me. Her diary was my lifesaver. She knew how I felt.

I shared the bedroom with three sisters. Dad had built bunk beds that flanked two of the walls in an L-shape. My head touched the lowest bed when I stood in the small play space underneath it. Not that I played much. I was seated next to the precious cupboard my grandad had made. He'd sawn off the end of an old sideboard, but hadn't cut it straight, so the edge of the door tapered to form a thin triangular hole at the bottom, but I didn't mind that. Bright sunlight streamed through the window and caught the gold padlock on the door. The key was always in my pocket. That lock was the only thing that stood between my personal things and prying eyes and hands that wanted to take ownership of my stuff.

I was crouched in the shadow created by a heavy black-out curtain, hoping I'd go unnoticed if anyone put their head around the door. A small bedside lamp with a low-watt bulb shone over my shoulder so I could make out the words in my book.

I'd not long arrived home from school and still wore my uniform, a black pleated mini skirt which my Religious Education teacher had pointed out was 'so last season,' a white shirt and navy and yellow striped tie. A wide blue headband kept my long auburn hair back off my face.

My parents were at work, which meant my two brothers were in a full-on war zone. When left to their own devices, all they did was fight. I could hear their shouts and screams from my place of refuge. One of my sisters tried to break up the fight, which was usually my job, but I'd flung my hands in the air and left them to it. It was a jungle down there.

I flipped open the book and found my page, stuck my thumb in my mouth and started to read. I crossed my heart and hoped my brothers would not kill each other before I got to the end of the next chapter. As I soaked into the words, the noise faded and I evaporated inside my favourite hiding place.

I thought I was hiding from the raucousness of my family life, but I now appreciate that the escape was from the noise of my thinking.

As the story seeped into and filled my mind, the fear, the anxiety, the feeling of inadequacy and of not being loved would fall away. Without realising it, I had escaped the storm of my thinking.

When I look back, even though I was afraid most of the time, I saw I'd found a way to take care of myself. I found a way to allow all my thinking to fall away and to come back to the peace and calm inside me.

What I used to think of as an escape, I now see as innate wisdom. Wisdom guided me to take care of myself, even though I didn't know yet that was how it worked.

Wisdom provided a way for me to get away from the hectic, boisterous, scared life I experienced through my own thoughts.

Wisdom brought me back to my true self.

5
A THORNY PERIOD

There have been times in my life when I've jumped into things with little thought. Like the time I decided to leave my job and start my own business. The idea came to me with a clarity that brooked no argument, and the decision was made in a nanosecond. I jumped right in with both feet and never once looked back. This jump was a success, but that's not always been the case.

Other times when I've jumped I've ignored a quiet little voice that said, 'Don't do it!' I jumped anyway and landed feet first in what looked like a bed of roses, but turned out to be a cesspit of epic proportions. I remember one such misguided leap as if it was yesterday.

Mark was my boyfriend of two years. I'd found out he was having an affair and had confronted him about it. Of course, he was vehement in his denial and indignant that I should accuse him of such a thing. I'd never known a man to be so blatant in his bare-faced lies. Even though I knew I was right, he convinced me I was in the wrong. He stood in front of me, in a pure wool camel overcoat that hid a multitude of sins.

"We could get engaged," he said.

The lounge of my cosy little house was cast in shadow. It was late evening and I hadn't switched the lights on when he arrived. He wasn't staying. The red brick and concrete fireplace was solid and bleak. The clock on the wall gave out a large clunk as it marked each second. I was cold, despite the full length peach fleece dressing gown that shrouded me from head to foot. I felt like a glacier on the inside and no amount of heat could thaw me out.

A voice inside of me said no, with the resonance of a flute, crowded out by the cacophony of a brass band. A film was running in my head. I imagined the ring, the house, the marriage, the happy ever after so many others had and I craved. I pictured the cessation of the eternal question; 'Why is a nice girl like you not married yet?' The frog turned into a handsome prince.

Mark stood looking down at me, an unlit cigarette in his mouth. His eyes bore into my soul and switched off my reason.

"Okay," I said.

That was it! I'd jumped. Even though the voice inside of me was adamant, the words that came out of my mouth sold me down the river.

The idea had intoxicated me. A part of me knew it was his attempt at control, but it was later I'd learn what a true master of emotional manipulation he was.

I'd landed with both feet and anchored myself in a bog that would take me ages from which to extricate. I'd blinded myself with the hope it would be something that, deep down, I knew it would never be. The smell was low level, but through the years it deepened, and the stench became stronger.

Sometimes there were roses offered as a token of love. An outward representation of the flimsy, whimsical pretence of love that was on offer.

It was only ever a single rose. The most expensive, the most lush looking, the deepest red rose, meant to represent a powerful impression of affection. He was a master of subterfuge and misdirection. My finger caught on the sharp thorn and in my innocence, I was convinced it symbolised the pain of true love.

The jagged barb sank its teeth in, inveigled itself, took root under my sensitive, soft skin. The poison, the pus accumulated as the rot set into this impassioned, impoverished love affair, based on an illusion.

That quiet voice of wisdom was there before I jumped, but I ignored it and jumped anyway. It did all turn out well in the end, but it was a thorny period in my life.

6

THE VENTRILOQUIST'S DUMMY

I'm a yes person. You know what I mean! I say yes, when what I really want to say is 'No.' What I really want to say is 'Let's do what I want to do for a change.' I want to say 'Fuck Off!' Instead I beat about the bush. I acquiesce. I push my wants and desires down to the bottom of the pile. Just once, I'd like to not bend to what someone else wants. Amongst the myriad of times when I've given in to keep the peace, one instance springs to mind.

I stood with Mark in the foyer of a new, multi-screen cinema that had opened the week before. It was the first Saturday night since we'd lived together that his daughter, Eloise, was with her mum. I knew he wouldn't be keen on the idea, but somehow I'd swallowed the glut in my throat and suggested we go out to watch a film.

"What film do you want to watch?" he asked, as if I had any say in the matter. I looked at the enormous television screens above our heads. Fifteen theatres, fifteen films, fifteen options, but it was Hobson's choice.

I watched the contorted facial features of the actors as they screamed and shouted to make themselves heard, but the volume was turned to mute.

We stood side by side. Mark was six feet tall, baby faced, with thick brown hair that curled up at the edges, hair that many a woman had wanted to run their fingers through. He wore jeans, and a starched white shirt, his unvarying weekend attire. Stale tobacco from his forty cigarettes a day habit emanated from his pores.

I was five feet two inches small, my red hair cut into a pixie style, with a feathered fringe. My hands stuffed deep into the pockets of my maroon puffer jacket. My arms felt like they were clamped to my body, my feet glued to the floor, and my jaw wooden as I rolled the options around in my mind. Titanic was the film everyone was talking about and the one I wanted to watch, but I didn't have a cat in hell's chance of him sitting through three hours of soppy romanticism.

Dozens of cheerful people chatted, and I could hear snippets of conversations. All of them making their choices. Starburst or Maltesers. Slush Puppy or Diet Coke. Nachos or a hotdog. I knew what I wanted, and I knew what I would get.

Industrial fluorescent lights blazed in the high, domed roof. The floor to ceiling windows, with the black night sky as their backdrop, reflected the activity within. Millions of dirty shoes and fingerprints had not yet dulled the polished chrome fixtures and fittings or the faux marble tiles with stuck-on arrows to direct the audiences. My heart pounded and my stomach churned as I weighed up whether to stand firm and be honest about what I wanted.

I was aware of the pressure of Mark's hand on the small of my back, the proprietary gesture that looked innocent to the casual glance but was there to remind me who was in control.

"How about Alien Resurrection?" I said. The ventriloquist's dummy had spoken. The wind had gone out of my sails. One act of courage in an evening was plenty. I wasn't brave enough to push my luck any further.

"Great idea," he said. "I knew you'd want to see that."

Of course I had the Starbursts when I wanted Maltesers, Slush Puppy instead of Diet Coke, Nachos instead of a hotdog.

I look back on those days and I thank God I am no longer in that relationship. I am no longer the ventriloquist's dummy. I recognised that was no way to live and was able to walk away. I thank God I met and married a man for whom my wants and needs stand equal to his.

7

I SHOULD HAVE SAID NO

Sexy, I am not. I have a hole in my sock where my toenail shows through. My cream fleece dressing gown needs a hot wash and my Ugg slippers are worn down at the heel. The smell would give a rugby team's kit room a good run for its money.

I don't need to be sexy. I don't need to put on an act and pretend to be something I'm not. I don't need to wear clothes that show off my cleavage, my legs, my ass. Gone are the days when I bend to how someone else thinks I should dress.

My ex-boyfriend wanted me to look a certain way, so that other men would drool at the sight of me, but he hated it when they did and then blamed me for it.

He wanted me to be something I wasn't, someone who would flaunt themselves, someone who liked to wear raunchy underwear, and do things I didn't want to do. He wanted someone who would take the abuse, be at his beck and call, whenever the mood took him and whether I wanted it or not. He liked nothing better than to degrade me.

He took away my soul and reduced me to the lowest common denominator, the scum of the earth. I hated him.

For what he did. For what he made me do. For stealing my innocence. For my shame.

I let him do those things. I didn't say 'No.' I let him mould me into something I wasn't. I put up with it for too long. I let him make me feel that way. I should have said 'No.' I should have stopped him, and left him long before I did.

Wisdom spoke to me, but I couldn't listen. I was too afraid. Too lost in thoughts that he'd told me I should believe. Too insecure to appreciate they weren't true. I believed him when he said I was selfish, ugly, a whore that no other man would want to touch with a barge pole and that I'd never manage on my own without him. His words struck a chord that had woven itself into my core decades before, and I stayed.

One day, wisdom refused to be pushed down. It made itself heard. Loud and clear, I heard something from deep within me say, 'Leave and leave now.' I ran with jet-fuelled shoes to a safe haven. A place where wisdom could not be clouded by a fog of despair and self-doubt, a place where my body once more became my own, where I could regain the connection to my soul. A place where 'No' is an acceptable and respected response.

PART II

I TURNED AROUND

Life changes
in an instant,
on the back of a new thought.

Although many realisations in my life have been gradual, there have been times when I knew I had seen something profound in an instant. Eureka moments, when a flash of awareness hit me like a bolt out of the blue. Lightbulb moments when I could see with perfect clarity in an instant. 'Aha' moments when my experience of life changed, even though at the time I couldn't even imagine how it would pan out. All I knew was something was different.

These are the moments when I turned away from the bars of the cage and looked in a different direction.

8
THE WORLD ALREADY KNOWS I AM HERE

As a child, I learned it was best to be seen and not heard, that if I expressed my opinions, there'd be repercussions. I learned not to stick my head above the parapet, to not speak up. I especially learned to keep angry thoughts to myself.

I hid myself away so I would be invisible. Think of how the eye of the storm is dead quiet and everything around it is in chaos. I was the opposite. From the outside you would see dead calm, but the eye, my thinking world, was in chaos.

With nowhere to escape, my thoughts grew louder and wilder in my mind and as a teenager, the storm turned into a tornado.

As an adult, I let the storm rip. I developed a reputation for my hot temper and I was proud of it. I knew people were intimidated by me, and I thought it meant I was strong. People would listen to me, pay attention. It meant the world knew I was here.

The turning point came when I was a leader of a large team. Dawn, my deputy, was my calm and balanced side-kick. She was wise beyond her years, and I respected her opinions. One day, we were having our annual appraisal discussion. We'd talked about how we worked together and Dawn had mentioned how useful it was that I gave her a lift to the office every day. It made sense as we lived near each other, but I was interested why she thought it was useful, in the context of our conversation.

"Dawn," I said. "Of course I'm happy to drive you, but why do you say it's useful?" My heart pumped less than half a beat before she said, "Because then I can make the team aware of whether it's safe to talk to you."

You could have knocked me down with a feather. We were seated in the corner office, on the fourth floor of a high-rise building. We were positioned in a ten to two o'clock position at a round, beech table. We were flanked by two large windows, which meant the room was drenched in natural daylight. It was one of those bright, cloudless days when there was nowhere to hide from the sun.

The many times I'd walked into the office in a temper flashed through my mind. All the times I'd raged at members of my team, or given people the silent treatment because I was in a bad mood. The times when the office would fall silent, heads bobbing down, eyes fixated on computer monitors as I'd walked through the office with a tornado raging above my head.

My Celtic looks; red hair, freckles, green eyes and Irish heritage, were how I'd defended my stormy temperament.

Dawn's sleek black hair fell in a soft bob around her face. She was still looking at me, her brown eyes unflinching.

"Thank you, Dawn," I said.

There wasn't anything else to say. What dawned on me (forgive the pun) when she said that changed my life. I decided there and then I would no longer be that kind of leader. Instead, I would be calm and well-balanced, the leader my team could talk to whenever they needed.

It didn't happen overnight, but a while later, an HR manager, on a visit to my office, said, "I wish I was as calm as you, Maria." There was no greater compliment she could have paid me.

It's not that I don't get angry these days. I still encounter stormy feelings, but they don't have the same power over me. I don't storm around in a temper because of them, ranting and raving at people, blaming them for my moods. Shouting at people no longer gives me any satisfaction.

The feelings are a barometer of my thinking that indicate my state of mind. When I get angry, it's often because insecurity and fear have taken over. When I drop that story, the need to shout will disappear. Yet the feeling of anger can be a driving force to help me speak up and defend a cause.

I can be quiet, and I can speak up. I find I am more likely to be heard when I am calm and reserved. I no longer feel the need to shout. The world already knows I'm here.

9
DID YOU EVER LOVE HER?

Somewhere along the line, I learned that love wasn't something you simply gave away to people. A person had to earn love and if they didn't deserve it, I wouldn't give it to them. That was my vow.

So I hid love. I put it in a place where I forgot where it was. I didn't realise that was what I'd done. It's one of those things an innocent child does to survive. It may look crazy now, in the cold light of day, but it made perfect sense from my child's perspective. Ash, my husband, and I had lots of conversations about my mum.

"Did you ever love her?" he asked.

We were in the lounge, on the sofa in our warm dressing gowns. It was early morning, and we'd been talking. This was the beginning of a routine that would become something of a ritual for us. The question had thrown me off guard. Nobody had asked me that before.

The late December morning sun shone through the window reflecting the warmth of the sunflower yellow walls. We'd been talking about love and how my mum hadn't done anything to warrant mine.

I look so much like her with my colouring and short stature. I used to have her short temper too, but that was a long time ago.

Did I ever love her? The answer seemed to be yes, but if it was, what had I done with that love? Instinct told me it was here somewhere.

An oversized Nordic Fir tree, heavy with red and gold baubles, dominated one corner of the room, filling the air with the smell of pine, cinnamon spice and Christmas."Oh my gosh, it's here," I said. "I found it."

I'd closed my eyes and gone straight to it. I knew where it was, hidden in a place deep inside me where I would never think to look and wouldn't stumble across it by accident.

That discovery was a life changer, although I was still reluctant to give love away. I'd stuck by that vow for so long. I'd lived with the belief for more than forty years, so breaking it was hard. Somewhere in my mind, the thought that love needed to be earned had left a residue.

I'd believed love was a commodity in short supply. I'd thought I only had a finite amount of love to give, and when it was gone, it was gone. I'd thought I had to be careful about who I gave love to, in case it brought me pain. I'd thought giving love to the wrong person caused my suffering. But I tell you now, that's where I got it wrong.

Withholding love caused my suffering. It's difficult to withhold love. It takes a lot of effort. To withhold love, to keep love locked away, I had to keep hold of a lot of old thoughts built up over many years. I had to accumulate more of the same kind of thoughts to back up, support and reinforce the original suppositions

tion that love was not something you gave away for free. I had to keep finding more reasons to hold love back.

To do that, I had to guard my love, like a soldier standing to attention outside Buckingham Palace. My eyes fixed ahead, my body immobile, my iron will focussed on one dot on the horizon, so I couldn't drop my shield and let love happen, even for a second. I layered an entire load of stuff on top of it, to keep it from showing up. All the effort bore me down. But it didn't weigh love down. Nothing can do that. Love is weightless and unconditional. The thought that love needs to be earned tricked me into a life-time of hard labour. Nobody told me differently. Others agreed when I told them love had to be earned. It's a common misconception. Why would you give love to people who don't deserve it?

Because when you hold it back, it doesn't hurt them, it hurts you. Love is who you are, and when you try to block it, when you hold love back, you're the one who suffers.

10
EGO UP TO ITS TRICKS

I'd started my business three months before, and my confidence was precarious. I was running an event for my first customer. It was day one of a workshop with a leadership team. The day had gone well, but after lunch there was a short period when things went pear-shaped. Two of the directors got into a war of words. They were savage with each other. If they were cave dwellers, they would have clubbed each other to death. Then, as swiftly as it started, it finished. All in all, it was less than five minutes. The two guys calmed down and we got back to the agenda.

For them, it was done with, but for me, the battle had scarcely got started. Every day for the next week, voices in my head ripped me to shreds. They told me the argument had been my fault. They questioned my capability, demanded to be told how I could let things get so out of hand. They judged my leadership skills, my ability to run a business, my training and coaching, my aptitude as a human being. They told me I should throw in the towel, that I had nothing of any substance to offer.

I thought the Managing Director would cancel the rest of the programme. Every time the phone rang, I jumped out of my skin thinking he was phoning to tell me what a failure I was.

A week later, I sucked up my embarrassment and worries and returned to the office for day two. The Managing Director was in the reception area when I arrived.

"Hi, Maria," he said. "Please come into my office."

It was a typical seventies' office building. The beige walls hadn't seen a paintbrush for years. Near the ceiling, damp patches caused the plaster to bubble and the paint to flake. Old brown stains speckled the wall near the coffee machine. This was a company that had bigger things to focus on than day to day housekeeping.

I was seated on a functional, black leather armchair in the reception area. My sweaty palms held on tightly to a smart, tan leather briefcase, which, in a flash of optimism, I'd filled with materials for the day. My face felt drained under the skin-toned foundation. My stomach a cement mixer with a full load. It churned, agitated, and threatened to spew its contents at any moment.

"Okay, thank you," I said. I clamped on a smile, gulped down a ton of bile and steeled myself for the guillotine that was about to fall.

I followed him into his office, and sat down on the large chair in front of his desk. I was a child hauled up in front of the head-teacher. Important looking paperwork with complex diagrams and notes covered the desk along with several coloured pens and a half-full cup of coffee. It was obvious he was a man who meant business. In the glass cabinet behind him was a host of awards. Cut glass bowls, wooden and metal totems all engraved with accolades for the successful firm. It was obvious he didn't need me.

"I can't tell you how much I'm looking forward to today," he said. "I've already seen changes in the team and it's been great."

I was speechless. My ego had done such a number on me!

It still tries to snare me sometimes. It's intimately familiar with my weak spots, my vulnerabilities, my triggers and it tries to needle its way in to make the tiniest of faults into a holocaust. I used to believe what it had to say, but these days, I am on to what icy ego is doing and it can no longer hold me in its grip. I don't pay it the attention or listen to it as much, so it doesn't paralyse me. I notice when it's up to its old tricks and then I get on with my day.

11
I LOOKED WITHIN AND DIDN'T LIKE WHAT I SAW

Busy is a constant state of mind for me. Busy is normal. Busy is who I am. I like being busy; it makes me feel like I have worth.

I was drinking a hot chocolate with a therapist friend of mine and we'd been talking about my busyness. She suggested we do a brief experiment. I'm always game for that.

"Imagine you're on your own," Mandy said. "No television. No music. No books. You don't have anything to do."

I was seated on her leather chesterfield, with clumps of stuffing coming out of the seams. Mandy had two house rabbits and it was their favourite chew. I could smell wood chipping from the cage in the corner. I wore a thick blue Arran jumper and ski socks under my denim jeans, but was still cold. She'd switched the heating on when I arrived, but the room hadn't warmed up yet. Mandy is as hot-blooded as she is warm-hearted and even on the coldest day, she wore light jeans and a short-sleeved t-shirt. Today's had 'Save the World' emblazoned across her chest.

My eyes were welling up. A tsunami of emotion threatened to drown me. I felt like I was suffocating and couldn't come up for air. It was a wave of hopelessness and despair. A light went out in my mind and darkness formed a shroud around me.

The sun shone through a window to my right and created a box of white on the linoleum floor that I yearned to step into, but I was paralysed. As I was drawn into the vortex, I could smell the chocolate and feel the heat of the mug cupped in my hands.

"OK." Mandy said, catching my distress. "Let's not do that." It was scary, and I didn't have a clue what the hell had happened.

It was several years later before I realised that I'd had a head to head with my self-created identity. A part of me, I believed, was unlovable and unlikeable, a worthless clod. A part of me I kept separate, alone and hidden. I'd looked at myself and didn't like what I'd seen.

I'd heard people say 'Look within,' advice given throughout the ages, from ancient philosophers, and religious scriptures to modern day gurus and writers. I'd also heard it said, I'm 'already what I'm looking for.' But I couldn't make head nor tail of that.

One bright morning, I was with Dicken Bettinger, my mentor, in his lounge in La Conner. I watched hummingbirds flit about outside; their vibrant heads flashed and flirted with me, diverting my attention away from Dicken. I didn't catch what he said, but it was something about our self-created identity, our ego, the part of ourselves that seems like it is who we are. He said that beyond that, deep within ourselves, is our true self.

I don't know if it was because I was transfixed by the lightning speed and beauty of the hummingbirds, but something slipped under my radar and into my heart. I heard 'Look within' in a different way. It was like I'd stumbled and fallen back into a part of me that felt alien, yet eminently familiar. I turned away from who I thought I was and found my true self.

I came to see my true self is not alone or separate, but a part of a greater whole. My true self is the seer of that other identity; it is the truth of who I am. I've haven't looked back since. What a blessing!

I still have lots to do, but the busyness has a different quality about it. I'm not busy because I need to run away and hide from something bleak inside of me. Sometimes I forget and I feel overwhelmed again, but then I remember and I know where to look. I turn about and return to my true self.

12
THE MAGIC OF UNDERSTANDING

I'm not sure I trust my memory anymore. There are certain stories that are common parlance in our family history, but we all have different versions of them. Dawn, the middle sister, wearing a green and black tartan cape and matching hat, fell into the river at Tamworth Castle. Dawn remembers that Sue, our younger sister, got a dunking in the River Tame, but there was no green and black tartan cape or hat. Sue remembers the river and almost drowning, and also a pink cape with a fur trim.

I remember other things, but when I analyse the memory, the logistics don't fit. I remember one bonfire night. Fireworks in the back garden. Catherine wheels, rockets and homemade toffee apples. I remember the house, the fence and Jack and Joyce, our next-door neighbours. Donned in a warm coat with a purple woollen hat with straps tied under my chin, I waved sparklers and created shapes in the air. I can picture the photograph taken at the time. In the photo, I am maybe three years old. We didn't live in that house, with that fence and those neighbours until I was eight. I remember half a story but forget the ending.

For much of my life, what I remembered most about my childhood was feeling horrible and unworthy. Scared. Alone. Unloved. Someone who deserved the harsh physical punishments I received. These painful memories tainted my life for decades.

When I began to understand the Three Principles, and started to see how I carried negative memories from the past, I could leave them in the past. I began remembering more happy times and pleasant feelings. It's weird, I know, but that actually happened. New memories surfaced, filled with love, happiness, and contentment. It was like all the pleasant moments had been put in the back of the wardrobe and forgotten, and learning about the Principles drew them out.

When I reflect on my childhood today, I see it in a different light. I realise I thwarted certain memories and inflated others. I carried the most negative of these with me, which contaminated my everyday experience.

As a young adult, I lived with a distorted memory of my past. I focused my attention on the moments of pain, hurt, and negativity. I had erased all the loving moments. Regardless of how bad our life is, there are always some of those. We don't remember because of where we focus our thoughts. My eyes brim as I remember one such moment.

We'd been to visit my grandparents. I believed they lived a hundred miles away. The truth is, it was only twenty-five.

Dad opened the car door. "Ria. Wake up," he said. "We're home."

We were parked on the street outside our small, terraced house. One house in a hundred, all side by side, a row of tin soldiers with their uniform sash windows and brightly painted doors of red and green and blue and brown.

The door of the beat-up Ford Cortina Estate was wide open. I was on the rear seat and could feel the icy bite of the arctic night wind on my face. I was snug in my lime green woollen hat, purple mittens and warm coat. A half-eaten lollipop was stuck to my lapel. It had dropped out of my mouth when I fell asleep. I wasn't ready to wake up.

I was four years old. Too big to be carried by Mum, but small enough to be lifted by Dad. I kept my eyes closed and pretended not to hear him.

"She's still asleep, Ange," he said to my mum. "I'll have to carry her." I could hear the laugh in his voice and her giggle in response.

He leaned into the car and swooped me out of the seat. I snuggled into him, breathing in the Old Spice aftershave, the Brylcreem in his hair, the scent of lorry grease on his clothes. His chin rested on the top of my head, and his muscular arms clasped around my body. Dad's broad chest pressed against my cheek. I could feel the tender love in his heart.

He carried me into the house and up the stairs. He placed me on my bed and removed my hat, coat, and mittens. All the time I pretended to be asleep. He tucked the bedcovers around me.

"Sleep tight, Ria," he said as he kissed me on my forehead.

"Night, Dad," I said, under my breath, with a contented smile.

When I stopped focusing only on the negative things that happened to me, I could see my childhood as a whole, rather than only the warts. As I did that, my present became a more pleasurable existence and memories like this surface more and more.

PART III

I LET GO OF THE BARS

I hold onto the bars
unaware
there is no cage.

When I reflect back, I see how my insights were a gradual progression, rather than one single 'Aha' moment. They were like a series of instances dotted here and there throughout time. A joining of the dots was happening, and a picture was emerging without me realising I was holding the pen.

Hindsight allows me to see how the patterns emerged, letting me pick out the thread as it wove patterns through my life. With the benefit of hindsight I can trust the patterns will continue into the future without me having to put in so much effort.

With hindsight I see this gradual joining up of the dots as my letting go of the bars of the cage. Here are some of those instances when the dots started to join up, and the pattern began to emerge.

13
MY STOLEN SOUL

Mark was good at a lot of things. He was a skilled salesman and could find his way easily around a computer. He was competent with practical things, like building a conservatory. But he wasn't good for me. As I mentioned before, he was a master of manipulation.

I knew he'd been unfaithful. I could feel the knowing deep in my gut, a place that is always to be trusted. But despite my assertion, he would not admit to the affair. He denied it repeatedly and then made it about me.

It was all in my imagination. It was obvious; I couldn't be trusted, so that's why I couldn't trust him. I had a bit on the side, so I thought he must have, too. I'd deceived him, so I pushed it back on him to make myself feel better. I couldn't accuse him without accusing myself. He would twist everything I said until my insides were knotted and I couldn't tell my arse from my elbow.

I stayed with him through all the affairs. Even though I didn't want to be there. I knew that as long as I was with him, I would never feel good about myself. Still I stayed. It was as if he had stolen my soul. The years rolled by.

At home, I was weak and subservient; at the office, I was strong and confident. At home I was downtrodden and bungling; with my team, happy and competent. At home I was scorned and disdained; in the workplace I was liked and respected. Mark told me I was selfish, inconsiderate, useless, incompetent, not trustworthy. I tried hard to prove him wrong and make him love me. No matter what I said or did, he would only see me the way he saw me. Because it wasn't about me.

A part of me, deep inside, knew that one day I would leave. Every day I would wonder if today was the day.

Today? No, I'm not brave enough.

Today? No, things aren't too bad.

Today? No, he's got a lot on his plate this week.

Today? No, we've got Christmas coming up.

Today? No not today either.

Day after day.

Month after month.

Year after year.

I'd believed I would never do it. I resigned myself to the fact I would invariably be too scared, that I was stuck with him forever. Then one day. I knew. Today was the day.

"I'm leaving," I said.

"Okay," he said. He didn't bat an eyelid. "Then you're leaving right now."

In the bedroom, the full-length mirrored wardrobe doors reflected the two of us in stand off position. I stood with my hands on my hips. It seemed the safest place to put them. I wore a charcoal dress, paired with a matching jacket and high heel, stiletto court shoes. I was the epitome of the professional business woman I would become, the second I walked out the front door.

My hair was cut short in a style that took little tending. My cheeks felt whitewashed underneath the full montage of foundation, blusher, kohl, mascara and lipstick, the mask I wore for my interactions with the outside world. This uniform hid the tear stains and the inner mould that infected my home life.

Mark wore a sharp, pin-striped suit, white shirt and grey tie. He looked good and for the longest time, the external façade had me hypnotised.

The sweet smell of furniture polish mingled with Hugo Boss Orange aftershave, last night's semen, and the dirty ashtray on the bedside table.

"Go now!" he said. I'd expected a showdown, a rage, a beating, anything but this quiet acceptance and forced exit. I didn't need to be told again.

I grabbed a handful of garden bin liners and stuffed my clothes into them, along with a couple of photos and some CDs. I was a woman possessed. I had to do it fast before fear changed my mind.

Within minutes, I'd stuffed my small, grey Vauxhall Nova car to the gunnels with everything I now owned. My hands held the steering wheel as tightly as the grip on my resolve. I was going to the office. I had no home to return to, no belongings to speak of, no apparent having it all, no illusion of a happy life. But oh my God, I was free!

I took a deep breath and felt every knot in my body come undone. All the weight I'd carried across my shoulders was set down. Every link in the ball and chain broke, and the shackles fell away.

I turned the key in the ignition and switched the radio on. '*Hit the Road Jack*' blasted out from the speakers. I smiled to myself and drove to work.

14

LOVE STOPPED ME

Ash was away in Boston, Lincolnshire for a few days. As he walked out the door, he said he thought I was glad he was going, that I was pleased to get a couple of days to myself. It's our little joke.

This time it struck a chord. He has a point. It's true. I do fine on my own. I don't pine for him when he's not here. And I miss him in my own way. I miss his quiet presence. The chat. The fun. The messing about. I miss his cuddle before I go to sleep.

I compare it to the previous relationship with Mark, when I couldn't wait for him to go away for a week, once a month. I lived for those precious few days when I had time on my own and I could be myself.

Every time he returned from a few days away Mark would ask me the same question. 'Why won't you marry me?' I'd been with him for ten years. We shared a house, a bed and a bank balance. He couldn't understand why I wouldn't say yes and he hated it. It wasn't that he wanted to get married, it was the fact that I didn't want to that got his goat. Even though I felt I had no voice in our relationship, in this I was resolute. I wasn't prepared to put the final nail in my coffin that would lock me in and put me under his full control.

So, in spite of the fact that I'd said okay to living together, something stopped me from tying the knot. I used to think it was fear.

Now I see it was the opposite. Love stopped me from doing that. Something deep inside me knew, if I married him, I could never untangle myself. Love and Wisdom work in mysterious ways.

Right from the beginning, I'd known I shouldn't be with him. Known that I'd have been better off on my own. All those years I ignored the small voice inside me. It may not have been loud, but it still managed to stop me taking one step too far.

Now I have another perspective. The time I spent with Mark was part of my life's learning. Once I'd learned the lesson, Wisdom told me, loud and clear, it was time to leave.

Wisdom ensured that when the time came, I wasn't padlocked inside the bars.

15

THE MASK WAS A PRETENDER

I was the strong one. The one you could always count on, the one who was happy and optimistic, easygoing and agreeable.

No matter what was going on in my life, I pinned on a brave face, a false smile, a sunny disposition. It was a façade, designed to keep everyone from getting too close to the real me. I wasn't worth knowing. I thought I wouldn't be liked if I was weak, or negative, or disagreeable.

My mind was a tumultuous, gruesome cesspit, and I feared if anyone caught a glimpse of it, they might turn away in horror. So I kept it closed in behind a mask. It was my normal.

There were times when I thought I was putting on another mask. I called it my 'professional demeanour' and I donned it when I was working with clients. During these times, I would have a different experience of life. I wasn't worried about what they thought of me, whether or not they liked me. The inner turmoil would die down and I would feel okay, happy even.

One day, the thought occurred to me that perhaps I wasn't putting on a mask, but instead I was taking one off. The idea intrigued me. I started to pay attention and notice the difference between the times when I felt okay, and the times when I didn't, but pretended.

I had worn a mask for most of my life and the 'professional demeanour' was not a façade, it was when I fell into being my true self. The mask I wore day to day had stopped me from being a full and active participant in the human race. It was the wrong prescription in a pair of spectacles. The lens blurred and distorted my vision, and diminished my view of life. I lived in a tunnel with a rabbit-holed view of the world.

I can understand why and how the mask seemed useful. But the mask was a pretender; it didn't deliver on its promise. I thought I'd bought a luxury item, but it was a cheap commodity. The whole, peaceful, loving part of me, my true self, was the one being sold out. The mask kept that part of me, the real me, hidden. More than that, it kept that part of myself obscured from me. It ensured I focused attention on my fragile, turmoil ridden ego. It held secure the idea that I needed protection, that I should be ashamed of myself, that I was a disgusting miscreant that should keep itself invisible. It closed down my experience of life.

Once I realised that, I dropped the mask to see what would happen. I let people in and allowed them to get close to my true self. I let people see my vulnerability, my weakness, and allowed people to help me. Over time, I saw that people accepted me, and were kinder than I thought. When I shared my frailty, people opened up to me with theirs.

I observed that while I was cloaked by the mask, it obscured my view of others. The mask drew my focus inward, so I saw only my suffering. It blinded me to the fact that others have their own turmoil, their own fear of vulnerability, their own façades.

When I dropped my mask, the masks others wear became more obvious to me. People were afraid of letting others in, afraid to expose their vulnerabilities. When people feel I have dropped my mask, it gives them the courage to let their guard down, at least for a while.

When I saw this, it was pivotal. The tsunami that raged within me settled into a gentle ripple. The need to put on a brave face diminished to a kind acceptance. The feeling of not being likeable or lovable had been replaced by a deep knowing of who I am at my core. I am love, and everything else is an illusion. I am no longer trapped in the blinkered vision of a mask. My world view has gained a wider perspective that brings an enjoyment to life that I never could have imagined.

Sometimes I forget and pick the mask up again, but not for long.

16

TOO SCARED TO PLAY

When I was a child, people thought I liked to be with the grown-ups. Adults said I had an old head on my shoulders. They were proud I was growing up so fast. Little did they know. They had no clue it was fear that kept me hanging onto their shirt tails. I couldn't tell you what filled me with such trepidation. I felt like I lived behind bars and somehow I was safe there, yet fear held me to ransom. I didn't know I was both captive and jailer at the same time.

Watching other kids play scared me the most. I remember one time, when I was twelve. On a sunny autumn afternoon the whole family had gone to Bradgate Park. My mum, dad and my five siblings. We'd stopped to watch a bunch of kids playing football on an enormous expanse of green. One of them kicked the ball, and it landed, like a surprise invitation, at my feet.

"Hey, pass the ball!" one boy said.

The park is an old country estate in Leicestershire, bequeathed as an open space for the community in 1928. Hundreds of people are drawn to its grandeur every day. A river zig-zagged through the park. Gnarled oak trees, standing proud for more than two hundred years, topped gold and red in the autumn sun. They marked the makeshift football pitch perimeter. The kids playing had dumped sweaters and coats in two piles to act as goalposts.

My breath was a cloud in front of me. A chill breeze bit my nose and tweaked my cheeks. I wore a hand-me-down dark mustard duffel and pink mittens held secure with a piece of wool that went up one arm and down the other. I could feel its scourge on the back of my neck. I wanted to kick the ball and join in the game, but my legs were like iron, held down by an industrial magnet attached to the bottom of my sensible shoes. My brother Tom stood next to me.

"Wuss!" he said.

He sneered at me as he kicked the ball right out from under me. He ran onto the pitch to join in the fun with his new mates. My shoulders sagged while the game carried on. I'd missed my chance. As usual, I was on the sideline of life.

I stopped seeing the game in front of me. I couldn't care less whether a goal was scored or which team won. I was fixed like glue in the midst of a head storm, hypnotised by a tsunami of negativity that drowned out the outside world. I was a captive of my mind, coerced and badgered by fear. The noise of the surrounding people was like a radio, with the volume turned down low. I was caught in the cacophony of my own thinking. Life was being lived around me and the weight of fearful thoughts froze me in time and space.

Fast forward forty years to a beach in Northumberland.

"Are you sure you're not coming, Maria?" Mandy said. Four of us had rented the old harbourmaster's cottage, six steps from the beach. I sat on the settee with my feet tucked underneath my bottom. The three of them had donned thick coats, woollen hats, scarves and Wellington boots. Mandy held a kite, stood on its end, that reached up to her shoulders. The plan was to make it fly.

I had a chick flick novel in my newly manicured hands, and a thick, chequered blanket at the ready to wrap myself up. An old man of the sea looked down from a picture frame above the mantelpiece. The two of us were set for some peaceful solitude. A grandfather clock ticked a slow, steady beat in the corner. The smell of soot and ashes and ocean brine permeated the room. A pine cone sat among the shells, stones and flotsam previous occupants had collected from the shoreline. "I'm sure," I said. I'd rather watch paint dry. "I want to finish my book."

When I was a kid, we had kites. I could never get them to fly. The last thing I wanted was the shame of failure hanging around my neck for the rest of the weekend.

The three of them left, and the room fell silent, like it had lost its heartbeat. I watched them through the panoramic window that gave a full view of the ocean. They skipped down to the beach like they were four, not forty something. The wind carried their laughter to a part of me that used to laugh a lot.

They unraveled the kite, then took turns holding the string, running with it, while another bellowed out instructions. It was obvious they had no clue what they were doing. Every time, the kite took a nosedive, but it just made them laugh all the harder. A sadness washed over me like a soft ocean wave.

I stood up so I could watch them better. As I did, I felt something loosen within me. Like a taut rope that secured a boat to the shore had slackened, like a deep sigh had released the air in all the locked-up parts of my body. Something akin to fear let go of me, or I let go of it.

I looked at my book, then out the window again. I'd thought I wanted some peace, but what I really wanted was some fun. I had no idea how to do that, but out there on the beach looked like a solid place to start.

I put on my burgundy Milan puffer coat and my new Hunter wellies, took a deep breath and closed the front door behind me. Mandy was the first to spot me.

"Woo-hoo! Maria's here!" she said. The three of them cheered.

I made an absolute fool of myself. There was no way the kite was going to do as it was told. When it was my turn, I ran up and down dunes, and I ran backwards. I tripped over my own feet and ended up flipped on my back like an overturned turtle. As I lay on the ground with the cold wet sand seeping into my core, I laughed. I laughed till tears poured down my face and my cheek bones hurt. I laughed till my ribs couldn't take any more. I felt a freedom I hadn't felt since... I couldn't remember when.

Somewhere along the line, I'd forgotten how to play. On that cold, damp November afternoon, I remembered.

17

CONCERT PART DEUX

It was autumn, 2017. My brother John had the brilliant idea to organise a charity concert. He was the drummer in a local band with five of his mates. 'Concert' is a little grandiose a word for it. He'd hired a hall for the evening and invited some other local bands and a few novices to entertain a gathering of friends and family and to raise money for charity. He also thought it would be a fine idea that Ash and I be one of the turns. I hadn't sung in front of an audience since one goddamn awful night some thirty years before.

As a child, I enjoyed singing so much that my primary school teacher, Sister Christina, had suggested I have my voice coached, but we couldn't afford it. When I was sixteen, I had the opportunity to sing one song at a concert with my first proper boyfriend. The song was Paul McCartney's Let it Be. I practiced until I was word and pitch perfect.

The time arrived and the purple velvet stage curtains had opened to reveal the two of us to the waiting audience.

"Are you ready?" Gary asked.

He was seated in front of a mahogany grand piano, a little to my right and behind me. He was dressed in a dark suit and black tie, more suited to a funeral than an evening of light entertainment at the Miners Welfare Social Club. I stood close to the front edge of the stage trying to peer through the wall of blackness in front of me. Out there was a large audience which included my mum and dad; my mum hoping I didn't make a fool of myself, my dad urging me to enjoy the moment.

I stood in my hour of darkness and prayed that Mother Mary would comfort me. There was a light that shined on me, but it was only the stage spotlights that formed a circle of doom around me.

Two blurry effigies crisscrossed behind me, the shadows cast by my body before being subsumed into the shade at the rear of the stage.

My eyes stung from salty sweat that streamed from my forehead blotching the black mascara I'd applied with so much care, only an hour before.

I could taste the heavy tobacco smell emanating from the crowd. My hair was going to reek of it later.

My gown was a boa constrictor around my waist and chest. The three-inch stiletto heels seemed ready to project me like a missile into a battle zone. My lips, now bereft of lipstick, felt as dry and cracked as the Sahara Desert.

This was my judgement day. My do or die. A chance to prove to the world I was worth something.

I gripped the song sheet with my fingers. The letters and words mixed themselves up on the page. The spotlight closed in and I couldn't see the paper. It wouldn't matter, anyway. The words were not the problem.

Gary's hands hovered above the ivory keys.

"No," I said. "I'm not ready."

Gary laughed and started to play the melody.

Fear scarified my voice. From start to finish, it was one long drawn out monotone.

I don't remember the audience's reaction. I don't remember running off the stage, although I'm sure I must have done. It's like my life started and ended in the eternity of those three minutes. I vowed I would never subject myself to such a trauma ever again.

So you can imagine my shock hearing myself say 'Yes' when John asked Ash and me to sing at his concert. I have no idea what possessed me! We chose three songs, which I practiced a bit, and I was sort of happy with how they sounded. Then it was the night of the concert.

We were on our way to the hall. "I'm not sure I want to do this," Ash said.

We were in the car, a white Vauxhall Astra. Ash was driving; I was next to him in the front seat. We didn't have to do it. We could back out. No one would be any the wiser. It was a dark night and heavy rain bounced like ball-bearings off the windscreen. The wipers struggled to keep pace.

I'd put extra effort into styling and curling my once auburn now ash-blonde hair. My brown boots, blue jeans and floral lacy blouse matched the Country and Western themed songs we'd chosen for our set. The volume of the radio was turned down low, but I could hear Dolly Parton singing 'You Can Do It.'

"You know something," I said. "I really want to do this." I didn't care how bad I was, or how off-tune I sang, I just wanted to get onto the stage and enjoy myself. I wasn't bothered about what anyone might think.

That's what I did. I remember so much more about the second concert. I remember the journey, the venue, the stage, the instruments, the technology, the lights, the people on the stage, my clothes, how I felt, the songs, and most of all, the joy. I remember the audience. Some watched, some joined in with the songs and clapped along with the music, and some didn't pay attention at all.

My voice was a series of bum notes interspersed with some sweet melodies. I laughed and clapped my way through the songs. I danced and shook the tambourine above my head, in front of me, beside me. I was light on my feet, exuberant, exhilarated, and elated all at the same time. No pin could burst this bubble of joy.

I was free of the demons that had held me back all those years ago. Free of the worry about what others would think of me. I no longer cared about being judged by the audience.

Most of all, I was free from the expectation I'd placed on myself to be perfect. I had stopped measuring myself against that impossible bar, freeing myself from my own self-judgement. I chose not to find fault with myself, which gave me the freedom and took away the fear. That allowed the joy of life to show up. The freedom opened up my senses and widened my perspective. Freedom was the difference between these two concerts.

18

CHANGE THE REEL

I slept till ten this morning.

What a complete and utter waste of a morning! I shouldn't have turned over for that extra five minutes when I woke up at seven.

I'll never recoup the time I've lost. Look at all the things I could have done in those three hours! It's true. I'm a waste of space. A lazy good for nothing who should never have been born. I serve no purpose. I'm a curse on the planet. A drain on resources. I contribute zilch. Who do I think I am?

It's not like I had plans. Ash and I had decided today would be a rest day. Things had been hectic for weeks; we wanted to take it easy. So I slept in. Big deal! Yet when I woke up, later than usual, the first thing I did was beat myself up. Thoughts like *I must have needed the sleep*, or *I didn't have plans for the day except to rest and now I feel rested* were not even a speck on the horizon. If I'd gotten up earlier, what would I have done? *I could've sat and done diddly squat.* At least I would have appreciated what I was doing. *I could've watched some trashy morning television, maybe. I could've relaxed and read a book.* I look around.

Time is marching on. The morning's half gone already. I can't sit here all day, gassing. I've got things to do. No rest for the wicked. I've had my chance and now I'd better get a shift on. That's what you get for sleeping late!

Here's my To Do List for the day:

- *Make breakfast (well, brunch now) then clear away and wash up afterwards.*
- *Tidy the lounge and vacuum round.*
- *Dust and polish.*
- *Clean the windows.*
- *Make the beds.*
- *Put some laundry in the washing machine (empty it later and hang it out to dry).*
- *Empty the bins.*
- *Go to the post office. (I need to package the parcels first.)*
- *Go to the supermarket to buy something for dinner.*
- *Wash up after dinner. (Dinner will be made for me, so that's at least one thing I don't have to do, but I'll clear up afterwards.)*

Hey wait up! This is my day of rest? When am I going to rest? Perhaps it was for the best that I slept for an extra three hours.

See how my conditioning gets me! The foundation was laid many years ago, and is so ingrained, so automated, so routed in my neural pathways, they still feature in my life. There's not anything wrong with them. They just exist, and I'm aware when they're the dominant feature of my thinking because I feel them. I feel the judgement, the criticism, the sense of being useless; it has a distinctive quality to it.

The feelings that come with this kind of thinking are like a barometer to let me know what's going on in my head. It tells me when the old conditioning has made its way into the film that is my life.

So, today I decide to change the reel.

Today I allow myself to be lackadaisical.

Today I choose to rest.

Now where's the remote control?

PART IV

DARK DAYS

A great white shark
in my underbelly,
feeds on what ifs.

Dark days. You know what I mean. Days that seem they've switched off the light at the end of the tunnel, ones where we think the end of the world is nigh. Days that last for weeks, months and even years. Days that feel like a curse, but more often than not, bring about a new lesson in life. We come through these dark days stronger, more resilient, more confident than we were before. Something within us changes during these dark days.

Here are some of my dark days.

The shit is hitting the fan.
What if it's not as bad
as it looks?

19
UNBEARABLE PAIN

My dad had been taken by ambulance to the Walsgrave Hospital in Coventry. He'd been square dance calling, his favourite thing to do ever, when he collapsed. My mum had travelled with him. My best friend Steve gave me a lift to hospital.

Dad had been conscious before they took him down to surgery. In pain, but alive and awake. We'd been told the operation would take hours, so we hunkered down for the long haul. I imagined how much Dad would enjoy this the next day. The jokes he would make of it, how he would lap up the love and hugs that we'd all bestow on him. He'd take it in his stride and make out it was all a fuss about nothing. How he'd love being the centre of attention. The three of us had been deposited in a family room to wait it out, but I'd nipped to the ladies' toilet, which is where a nurse found me.

"Are you John Iliffe's daughter?" she said.

The dark green, graffiti sullied, toilet doors were closed on empty cubicles. There was only me, and the nurse who'd copped for the midnight shift. Florescent tubes hummed and gave everything a sharp edge. The marble tiled floor was sterile. The smell of disinfectant whilst pungent, couldn't hide the smell of illness, disease, and hospital death.

I'd thrown on the crumpled jeans and jumper I'd worn all day after I'd received the call from Steve. The phone had woken me up and I was reluctant to leave my dreams and my warm bed. My mum was inclined to make a mountain out of a molehill when it came to illness, but something in Steve's voice compelled me to move.

The nurse stood in front of me in dark purple uniform with white piping and sensible loafers. Her watch was pinned upside down above her right breast. There was something in her eyes I didn't want to acknowledge.

"I'm so sorry," she said.

My legs went to mush. I let out a gasp. The globe ground to a crushing halt on its axis.

"No!" I cried out.

A dagger hit my heart and ripped me wide open. I was hung, drawn and quartered in a single sentence. My body felt crushed, impaled on a stake, and seared with a full body branding iron, all at the same time.

My mind could not comprehend the intensity of the pain.

I didn't think the pain could get any worse, that I was already at the limit, but it turned out this was just the start. As reality hit home, the agony would strike me again and again. When I broke the news to the rest of my family. When I told my friends. When I registered his death. When we arranged the funeral. Every time, another stab to my heart.

I'd go to the office and forget for a few hours, then I would remember and it was like being hit full on by a bullet train. I'd fall into the bliss that was sleep and forget for a night, then wake up in the morning and be hit again, full force. I'd go for a night out with friends and be entertained and distracted, then on the way home I'd remember again and fall back into the abyss.

I didn't think about how to bear it. I just did. I had no choice. What occurred to me was to keep on doing the daily, normal things that I did before Dad died. Get out of bed. Go to work. Have dinner. Meet friends. Watch TV. Go to bed. Sleep. Wake up. Put one foot in front of the other, one step at a time. Like an automaton. A robot. A human being trying to get by in life with the weight of unbearable pain.

Somewhere along the line, after my dad died, the planet cranked itself up. It groaned and screeched, like a rusty old engine, and then, reluctant and begrudging, it started to turn again. My world had shifted on its axis and I had to get used to the new order. It would always feel like I was missing a vital part, that I had to operate without. I was not okay, but I knew the pain I felt was not all of who I am. There's something about knowing this that helped me to learn how to live with the pain instead of trying to avoid it.

20
DEPRESSION

I lived alone. I'd taken to sitting in one place in the lounge for hours on end. Walls that once were sunflower yellow, armchairs red and gold, carpet soft oatmeal, all seemed monotone. The room was lifeless, like it had been touched by death's own icy, crooked finger.

Each morning I woke up to, *Oh God, not another day!* I'd struggle out of bed like a landlocked whale, and shuffle downstairs. By the time I reached the bottom of the stairs, I was exhausted.

One morning, I dropped the full force of my weight into a seat in my dreary, grey lounge. I stared at a grey feather on the rug amongst the muck and the dust. I couldn't remember the last time I'd vacuumed. My life was one slate grey mess.

I may have been in my pyjamas, or dressing gown, or joggers and a sweater that I'd probably worn for weeks. Who knows what I'd been wearing? I don't. I don't remember getting dressed. I don't remember taking a shower, brushing my teeth or my hair. If I stunk, I wasn't aware of it. My body didn't exist. I don't remember eating. My mouth tasted charcoal grey.

The days were a grey reel. Spring, summer, autumn, winter? Who knew! Only the cloud existed.

One day, something inside urged me let some light into this cold dark space. I hauled myself up and heaved one lead-weighted foot after the other to the window. I opened the curtains. The day was heavy with grey, insipid, don't give a damn, couldn't care less sort of clouds.

A tree stood alone in my front garden, stripped of its riches, its nakedness like poverty on display. No way to hide its embarrassment. If the tree had cheeks, they would have blushed red. If it had eyes, they would have cried in shame. Finger nails? They would have been chewed to the quick. Its nerves, torn to shreds. To the rest of the humanity, the tree was nothing; people walked by, oblivious to its turmoil. But I understood.

Three people knew about my impoverished existence. A therapist I talked to twice a week who invited me to dig deep and swim around in all the awful, insidious feelings I'd locked inside me. I spent most of the time with him in tears. The other two people were my friends, Ken and Jenny, my surrogate parents. I would visit them on my way home after the therapy sessions.

Ken would offer to fix some household problem for me, like a dripping tap, or put up a shelf, or clear the garden of weeds before leaving Jenny and me to talk.

Mostly, Jenny would hold my hand and listen. She asked no questions; she didn't try to fix my problem. She stayed with me until I'd exhausted myself. Then I would pick up the weight of my despair and carry it back home. I didn't notice that each time, it was a little lighter.

One day, I noticed the sun was shining. The tree had fresh green shoots on it that would soon become leaves of life and colour. The grey was a little less dense.

One day, I smelled the heady aroma of hyacinths that had somehow materialised in a vase on the mantelpiece. My mouth watered as if it yearned for something sweet and succulent. I heard the tick of the clock and noticed the time of day. Where had those hours gone? Those days, weeks, months?

One day, I remembered that I dance, something I'd not done for ages. Yet before the cloud had descended, dance was my passion. Something told me to get up, get myself out, and go to a dance.

The cloud passed. When it was my world, it was my world forever. The idea the cloud might dissipate of its own accord had never occurred to me.

For the longest time, I wondered what it was that got me up in the mornings. What told me to seek out a therapist and afterward, visit my friend? What reminded me I love to dance? What it was that returned me to the land of the living?

Later, I found out I have an inner knowing that navigates me through life. A light that shows me the way, even when I'm not aware of it. I understood I possess an innate wisdom that is in play whether I perceive it or not. This is what guided me.

Storm clouds do still gather in my life, but I don't get caught up in them like I once did. All clouds pass by, and there's a special part of me that shines a light no matter what.

21
GINGER URCHIN

I'm having a bad day! Lovely things in life like blueberries, children's toys and fancy necklaces fall prey to the all-encompassing umbrella of gloom. Dark thoughts churn up like a river of mangled and frayed carpets. Benevolent kisses get tossed aside and all that's left is cranky, churned up, chilling anxiety and despair.

Solid structures in my mind dissipate and crumble as hope and faith become empty echoes of distant prayers. Hope and faith become words of dubious comfort, peevish triggers of crabby disbelief.

I want to believe that all will pan out. That this anguish will depart tout de suite, as quickly as it arrived. I hate this feeling of not being in control of my fate, this not knowing what will become of me. More like I hate these projections of catastrophe, looking so real and then filling me with dread.

I watch it happen and I'm helpless in its vice-like grip, its aggressive, hard-nosed determination to congeal me in confused consternation and depression. I fall prey to the stampede of frenzied agitation in my mind. I have no choice, no option, no frigging free will to laugh and dance on my own tombstone, sing Glory Hallelujah and thanks be to God for this curse, this thing that is tantamount to a blessing in disguise.

It will simmer me into some kind of euphoric lightning bolt of a eureka moment and transport me on a rainbow filled with chocolate delights and rhubarb and custard treats.

Angels' wings will lift me high above the moon's pockmarked smile and multi-coloured, striped ponytails will swing-dance to crescendos of music that pulsate and build for dramatic effect. The air will be filled with fervent hope and genuine faith in spite of all indicators to the contrary.

Even though the churlish wolf lurks in the lofty barrage of coarse and clumsy thinking, and shame festers within, the genuine ginger urchin bounds into a bounty of upper-most fine fettle.

The thought police do their best to keep me down, but hope and faith are too bright. Hope and faith are two beacons that keep me going. There is no putting out those fires, they always light up the way.

22
I'M NOT A NICE PERSON

It wasn't that long ago that I made a sport out of finding fault in others. I called it gossip. There's no harm in a bit of banter, now is there? My friend and I would watch people, look for their faults, and then rip them apart. Not to their face, of course! We would pooh-pooh them for anything; they could be too fat, or too thin. It could be the awful clothes they were wearing. We would question whether their partner was too young or too old. We would ridicule the way they danced, the way they talked, the way they acted. It was our way. No, it was my way of feeling better about myself. I can't speak for my friend. Maybe it was her way of being my friend.

If I could get one over on another person, feel like I had an upper hand, then maybe I would feel positive about myself. If I could look down on others, it must mean I was better than them. If I could find something lacking in someone else, maybe I wouldn't notice what was lacking in me.

Believe me, whatever judgement or fault I found in another person, I found a hundred-fold worse about myself. I was stupid. I was selfish. I was ugly, fat, lazy. I wasn't useful enough, clever enough, pretty enough. I was not and never could be, enough.

It's a testament to how I feel differently about myself. I've remembered who I am, underneath my thinking, and I'm not the broken, imperfect, unlovable, unlikeable being I thought I was. I realise I have always been okay. I do not need to judge other people to feel good about myself.

I wish I could say that since I've seen the light, it doesn't happen anymore, but just yesterday, it happened. I was on the bus to Leicester. A woman had clambered on and plonked herself down on the seat across the way. I raised my eyebrow. She was a big woman, to say the least.

She was weighed down with several chock-full plastic carrier bags that had seen better days. Her emerald dress with large red flowers was pulled taut across her sizeable bosom, and rode up at the front to expose corpulent, chafing thighs. Thick, black, opaque tights struggled to cover gelatinous knees. The laddered lycra scrunched around her plump ankles. Her long dark hair, peppered with pewter streaks, looked greasy and matted. Mascara and kohl had blotched around her eyes. Even from across the aisle, the odour suggested a body that hadn't been near a shower for any number of days. The diesel fumes from the bus didn't help.

'She looks like something the cat's dragged in.' The words came into my mind before I could stop them, laden with distaste and damnation. They were there before I had a chance to do anything about it. Guilt for my thinking slapped me round the face like a wet kipper. This woman was a stranger. I had no clue of her history or what her life was like, yet here I was, judge, jury and executioner in my little tower of self-righteousness.

The bus engine chugged. The sun flickered and cast shadows like a monochromatic cinema projector inside the bus. We trundled along the country roads. I smiled at the woman as she caught my eye, the judgement and criticism forgotten.

Nowadays, when I experience these kinds of thoughts I don't pay attention to them. I don't find beliefs to line up behind them to make them true. I don't give the thought life by believing it. I no longer need others to be less than, in order for me to feel good.

Having a judgmental thought doesn't make me a bad person, so I'm careful not to pile on more judgmental thoughts about myself. Still, these old habits do return to test me.

When I don't pay them attention, they do what all thoughts do. They pass by. When they do, I can see the true self of the person, their innate beauty, and love them without judgment and without reservation. In doing that, I also see my own beauty, and I can love myself, too.

23
A CHOCOHOLIC

I love chocolate. Like a baby loves its mother's nipple, like the Greeks who drank the ambrosia of life. Like if it's the last thing I eat on this mortal coil, I'll die a lucky woman.

But look at the size of me. It's six parts habit and half a dozen parts sugar addiction. I know how it works. I eat sugar, then I crave more. I indulge the whim and put on weight. I look in the mirror and don't like what I see, so I stop looking. In my mind's eye I am young and slim and then I'm shocked when I glimpse my barrel-like grandma looking back at me. I've become her even though I vowed I wouldn't.

At the supermarket I say to myself; 'No chocolate today' and then at the checkout, there's a giant size Cadbury's Dairy Milk in the trolley. I pay for it and take it home. I like my chocolate cold, so I have a special box for it in the fridge.

Sometimes I don't succumb to the urge to buy. But then later, when I'm sitting in front of the television, I regret that decision. Like last night. I knew there was no chocolate in the house because I had bought none, yet I had to look, anyway. Just in case there was a lone square hidden behind the coleslaw.

I yanked open the fridge door saying "Chocolate." My mind was feverish as I scoured the shelves. I stood in my grey fleece pyjamas that made me look like the Pillsbury Dough boy. The fridge hummed at me in defiance. The kitchen was in darkness, but the fridge light showed me up. The box was empty except for a lone cherry tomato.

"Now what?" I said, and slammed the door shut.

I mulled over whether to go to the corner shop to buy chocolate. The shop is open till 10pm every night and my pyjamas could double as a track suit.

Chocolate cogitated in my mind in a mire of guilt, self-condemnation and desire. I shouldn't have chocolate. I eat too much chocolate. I'm too fat. I love chocolate. God wouldn't have created delicious chocolate unless I was supposed to enjoy it. I could get a small bar and eat one piece, and that would be ample. Plus I needed the exercise. I could walk to the corner shop and back again and that way I've killed two birds with one stone.

I went to the shop and bought the chocolate. The first square was divine on my tastebuds, like the elixir of life. I sat on the sofa and watched TV. When I looked down, all that was left was an empty wrapper. How had that happened? I'd eaten every bit and not even noticed.

It's funny; I can use the power of thought to convince myself to eat chocolate, too much of it, too often. I can convince myself to go to the shop to buy more, then eat it, not even taste it and then pay the price of weight gain, and yet I can't seem to use the power of thought to convince myself to leave it alone.

24

MONEY WORRIES

I worry about running out of money. It's a blind spot. I make up stories where I lose everything I've worked for my whole life. I don't deserve what I've got and I've got it coming to me.

Lucifer carved a black marbled cross into my soul when he staked his claim on my life. He's the arcane lover to whom my fruitless, inconsequential life is beholden. He allows me all the trappings but taunts me with the threat he'll take it all away. I feel it in my core. I know it's nonsense but it doesn't stop the idea forming in my head. I blow it up out of all proportion and for a while it paralyses me.

My bank balance was close to the red. I'd made two phone calls to chase overdue invoices and I was in a right stew. The universe had conspired against me. Neither company had any record of the invoice and couldn't tell me when I'd get paid. I was already in a two and eight before I made my last call.

"I'm sorry, that invoice is not in the system." Margaret said. She was a member of the accounts team for one of our biggest clients. I was at the kitchen table, sat on a dining chair that had gotten more uncomfortable as the day wore on. My Bose headphones were tight on my head. Her voice echoed like Dolby surround sound in my brain.

A MacBook was open in front of me, the screen displaying overdue invoices in our accounting system. The list was longer than ever.

I was opposite the patio doors that lead out to our small garden. A bullfinch was on the bird feeder, with his pink chest puffed out. I envied him his freedom from man-made worries.

The coffee in my hummingbird decorated mug had gone cold. Next to the cup, an elastic band, that snapped when I'd stretched it too far, whilst waiting on hold on a previous call. Andre Rieu played a jaunty waltz in the background. "Would you like me to send it again?" I said with a forced smile.

It was out of my control. Sand sifted through my fingers, no matter how hard I tried to keep hold. It was one of the hazards of running a business. I couldn't count on when the money would come in. With each call, my stomach had sunk further into the mire. I went from living in our cosy detached house to sleeping in a cardboard box, in a cold, dark, shop doorway, with only a grubby blanket to keep me warm.

I'm used to it. It's an old habit. I wish I could kick it so I didn't have to suffer the consequences. But no matter how much I understand the nature of thought, this anxious thinking just doesn't go away. It still catch me unawares. I can be having a perfectly good day and then... WALLOP! It's like my lungs collapse and my heart slams on the brakes. It's what death feels like, I imagine. Or a stroke. Or an aneurism. I wonder if it's how Dad felt when his heart burst and sucked the life right out of him.

When I have this thinking I feel like I'm dying. This is the moment it's gonna happen. The moment when the rug is pulled out from under me. I didn't deserve any of it anyway. The deal was an Anne Frank life, but somehow I ran past the finishing post and carried on. My luck's going to run out sooner or later.

"Thanks," Margaret said. "I'll get onto it straight away."

The crazy thing is, I knew she would. When fear gets me, when the dread happens, that 'my life is over' thought moves in and settles down. I forget I've liaised with Margaret for a long time now, and she always does what she promises.

Later that evening, I noticed that the worry feeling had disappeared. It had vanished in the same way it had arrived. On the back of a new thought.

PART V

I SEE THE DOOR IS OPEN

When the darkness is gone,
only then I see
the light that guided me.

The door to the cage of my life has always been open. While I held onto the bars, and looked in the other direction, I was blind to the truth. As I turned, I could see that the door was open, but there was a part of me that couldn't quite believe it. I thought that if I were to head towards the door, it would shut in my face. I had to get used to the idea that the door was open, was going to stay open and I could walk through it.

Now obviously this is a metaphor, but it took a while to see that a fresh experience of life was ahead of me and all I needed was to be open to the possibility of freedom.

25
MY MUM WASN'T MATERNAL

My mum thinks she was the worst mum in the history of the human race. I was the main protagonist in that story. I did everything to convince her it was true. I let her know plenty of times, if not in words, in deeds. She knew what I thought of her as a mum and it wasn't nice or pretty. I was self-righteous about it. I thought I was justified in my opinion.

Once I started to have insights about Mind, Consciousness and Thought, everything I thought and believed to be true about my childhood proved to be built on unstable foundations. As I realised how I'd carried negative thoughts from my childhood into adulthood, I started to see my childhood was not what I'd always believed it to be. The foundations crumbled, and the walls fell down.

I saw a different perspective about what life was like for my mum, and it shook me to the core. All the things I'd judged and criticised her for now became reasons to praise. As a mum she had done the very best she could with the limited resources available to her. She worked hard to set me up to have a good life, at the expense of her own comfort.

My mum once told me she wasn't maternal.

Well now, I'll show you she was and to quote Elizabeth Barrett Browning, "How do I love thee? Let me count the ways."

1) My mum had six children. She had no favourite.

2) She wanted for us what she didn't have for herself.

3) She made sure we had the opportunity for an excellent education. When she was a child, she moved all around the country. She went to fourteen different schools. She wanted something different for us and she gave it to us. Not only that, it had to be the best school.

4) She provided a stable home. Ditto. One school, one home. It meant leaving my dad in Germany to return to the UK. That was a price she was willing to pay.

5) She made sure we had plenty of food on the table. We never went hungry. Every Friday night we had fish and chips from the chip shop. It was under the guise of a Catholic tradition, but for us, it was a treat.

6) We had enough clothes to wear and on the rare occasion when she could afford it, we had new clothes. Yet we always had new shoes. Expensive shoes. Clarks shoes. "I don't want your feet to be impaired by other people's footprints," She'd say. She was adamant we wouldn't stand in someone else's track.

7) My mum fought in our corner. If we'd been picked on at school, or the teacher had done us an injustice, she would be quick to defend us. Still, she was quick to reprimand us if we'd done wrong. These days I am thankful for that, too.

8) She ensured we had lots of adventures. That is priceless. I have many happy memories of so many places: Woburn Abbey, Wicksteed Park, Bradgate Park, Beacon Hill, Bambi at the cinema. Bradgate Park is still my most favourite place.

9) Christmas and birthdays we had lots of presents. We all had one, brand-new bike each. We had the same number of presents, the same amount of money spent on each of us, the same volume of love and kindness bestowed.

10) Easter, Halloween, Fireworks night: She made them special. Easter eggs, apple bobbin', toffee apples, sparklers and fireworks.

11) Camping and caravan holidays. It meant she had to put herself at the mercy of her own parents, but she would do that so we could have fun.

12) As we got older, there were piano lessons, gymnastic lessons, drum lessons, guitar lessons, driving lessons. She scrimped and saved and went through hard times, so she could pay for these.

13) Most of all, my mum encouraged us to be independent, to make our own way, to be different.

Someone who was not maternal would not have done these things. She wouldn't have cared. We'd have been dirty, unclothed, uneducated. Neglected. God knows I would not have turned out to be the person I am today. A decent, kind person, someone who has made a positive difference in the world. I wouldn't be the me I am now if she hadn't been maternal.

After a lifetime of making it very clear what a bad mum she was, I want her to know in no uncertain terms this is not true. What I said in the past should be disregarded. She was an excellent mum, to me, my two brothers and three sisters. I want her to know I am grateful for everything she did for us. I am so grateful that she is my mum. I wouldn't swap her for anything.

26
1994 - THE YEAR OF LOSS

A lot of water has gone under the bridge since my nan died in 1994. In a few unbearable, short years, I lost her, my dad, my other two grandparents, and Steve, my best friend.

Long before Nan died, I dreamed I was at her funeral. Tears were a river that couldn't be dammed. I was inconsolable. I loved her so much, how she forever had a smile for me. I loved how she refused to have her birthday lunch with anyone else. She would get me to peel oranges for her because she loved them, but hated to peel them. I loved how she would talk about Tom, her husband, my grandad, whom I had never met, but whose mannerisms and characteristics I had inherited. Nan always had time to sit and chat.

In my dream I could see the coffin bearers like ants on the horizon, near the top of a hill. Nan came to me and told me not to be sad, that she was happy now. She was with Tom, after missing him for nigh on forty years. She said I should be happy for her, being where she wanted to be. When I woke up, actual tears streamed down my face.

Now it was her funeral. This time it wasn't a dream. It was unbearable. I couldn't imagine not seeing her again, not hearing her voice, not sitting by her side while she played her beloved piano. There would be no more oranges to peel. Life without her Tinkerbell laugh, beatific smile and lit up eyes when she saw me, was unthinkable. I couldn't imagine her birthday without our traditional birthday lunch followed by a walk in the park.

"We're here to celebrate the life of Thirza Jane," the priest said.

We were in a fourteenth century sandstone church. The smell of incense had a hay fever effect on me. Sunlight refracted into prisms through the mosaic glass windows. The pews cold and dark, were as ancient as the church. Knitted, crocheted and cross-stitched kneeling pads, handmade by the Women's Institute, were at the feet of the congregation, ready to soften discomfort as they fell to their knees in prayer.

The light oak coffin stood on makeshift legs in the centre aisle. The handles like polished mirrors. The remnant of a yellow duster was caught on the corner of the brass name-plate. Nan smiled at me from the filigree photo frame that sat on top of the coffin, her face blurred by my tears.

My eyes were vivid turquoise. They turn that colour when I cry. My lips were cracked and sore from biting back the grief. She'd left instructions for bright clothes and no floral tributes. *Flowers were for the living,* she'd said. I'd put on a plain navy dress and jacket and held a single red rose in my hand. It was the closest I could bring myself to honour Nan's wishes. I imagined her in the closed coffin. I pictured her as I'd seen her in the chapel of rest, in a pink lace gown. One she'd never have been seen dead in, when she was alive. I worried about whether she could breathe in the sealed box.

"Please be seated," the priest said.

He started the service. I was oblivious to the words. My eyes were fixated on the coffin, but my mind was elsewhere, flashing through the wonderful times we'd spent together. Her birthdays were among my favourites. One in particular, stood out.

"Let me buy you a Gerberis, our Ria," she said. I loved that she insisted on calling me Ria, to my mum's eternal consternation.

It was the birthday after I'd moved into my first house. She hadn't felt up for our usual walk after lunch and had suggested the garden centre instead. We stood in front of a raised stand, covered with dozens of Gerberis in pots. A glory of red, orange, purple, violet and green. The flower was one of Nan's favourites. In her hand was a white embroidered cotton handkerchief and a bright yellow flower. It matched the sunshine and brightness of her smile.

"Let me buy you this for your new garden," Nan said.

In the cold of the church, I smiled, despite myself.

The priest invited us to sing Thirza's favourite hymn. The congregation stood. The organ wheezed into tune and the choir began to sing. The words filled the church. They filled my mind and body. A feeling of love and peace washed over me. The words 'On a hill far away' echoed and filled the old stone church, from the cold flagstones and foot-worn tombstones, to the beautiful, bright and colourful stained glass picture windows, and to the painted eaves criss-crossed with solid old beams. I didn't realise *The Old Rugged Cross* was her favourite hymn.

I don't know what happens after death. I hope there is something after this life. When my uncle died, the first family death I was aware of, I could feel his presence, like he was watching me. I felt him for several days after he died; then he disappeared. After Nan died, in the days before her funeral, I looked for her. I thought if anyone would come back to look after me, it would be she. But the draw to be with Tom was too great. No matter how hard I prayed, she didn't come near me. I felt abandoned.

As the music filled the church, the words of the hymn registered in my mind and the dream flooded back to me. She hadn't deserted me or abandoned me. Nor had she left me to suffer on my own. She was here with me as surely as if she were alive, telling me she was okay, she was where she wanted to be, reassuring me I didn't need to be sad.

I still don't know what happens after death, but it appears to me there is some essence of the person that continues after this physical body dies. I have felt my nan, and my dad and the people I have loved and lost with me as surely as if they'd been in their physical body. They have spoken to me and guided me often in my life.

Nan left me that dream as a gift to hold on to, as surely as she'd given me the Gerberis on her birthday. I could say goodbye in full, certain in the knowledge that, wherever she is now, she is happy and where she wants to be.

27
DYING AND REGRET

I think more about death these days. My death. I wonder how it will happen. Will I be on an operating table with surgeons fighting for my life? Will I drown - my worst fear - and if so, will anyone try to save me? Will I die in my sleep? No fuss. No drama. No spectacle.

I wonder if I will fight to maintain this existence, or whether I will welcome death as a blessed relief. Will I even notice leaving this body?

What will it feel like? Will I be scared? I wonder if my regrets will mean anything. As a rule, I don't do regrets, but one springs to mind. It was 1982. I was in a Mark & Spencer's dressing room, trying on bridesmaid dresses for my best friend's wedding.

"Let's talk about my hen-night," Stef said from outside the curtain.

The cubicle was flooded with harsh fluorescent lighting. The smell of new clothes and smelly feet left a bile taste in my mouth. A chewing gum wrapper was caught up in dust, and loose fibres congregated in a corner. There was no marketing psychology in those days.

I was trying on a pale beige chiffon dress with white polka dots. It had a pretty scalloped collar, white buttons, and full skirt. I looked at myself in the full size mirror and hoped she'd say no to the dress, but I knew she would love it.

Stef and I had met in our first year at secondary school. We were the two shortest girls in the class and we got on like a house on fire from day one. We became joined at the hip. We used to sing 'Black is Black' at the top of our voices in the playground on a daily basis. Seventies elevator music played in the background.

"Hold on," I said.

I pulled the polyester curtain to the side so Stef could look at it.

She stood with one hand on her hip, her trademark stance. She had jet-black hair with a wayward curl and eyes that looked like a Caribbean ocean on a clear day. Her other hand hung at head height because she'd hooked her elbow on the hanging rail that held ten other garments I'd already tried on.

"Oh, my gosh," Stef said. All thoughts of the hen night disappeared in her delight with the dress. I was off the hook for now. "Yes, that's the one. Don't you just love it?"

The problem, other than the dress, was that I'd already told my boyfriend we'd go to a party on the same date. I knew it would upset Stef, but in those days I put my boyfriend first. I told myself she wouldn't mind, that her hen night was a simple meal out and we could do that any time, so it was no big deal.

And that's my one regret. I never went to Stef's hen night. I went to the party with Ken instead.

I wonder if that one regret will taint the moment of my death. Will I beg for forgiveness, or the opportunity to live that one night again so I can put it right? I wonder if, when I leave this body, that one choice will make a difference in the grand scheme of my life.

28

IMAGINED MISDEMEANOURS

I dream this book has gone viral. Every man and his dog wants to read it. I can't print it fast enough to keep up with demand. And as much as I am thrilled and giddy with excitement, I am scared to let people close to me read it. I want to write a disclaimer that family and friends are not allowed to read it. I know, weird right? And all sorts of crazy. But this stuff is so personal.

The truth is, I don't want my mum to read some stories. I fear she'll read the negative and ignore the positive, and the chances are, it will upset her.

"Don't you think she's had enough pain in her life?" I ask myself and the answer that comes back is: "Well, you caused most of it."

I did, truth be told.

As a child, I wasn't a rebel or defiant. I wouldn't shout at my mum or fight with her. I was a good girl. I would do my home-work, the housework and look after my brothers and sisters, like I was told, but I would simmer inside.

I was scared of my mum. Scared of her anger, and her wooden spoon. Scared that she would report my misdemeanours to my dad, which would incur the dreaded leather belt.

I thought she didn't love me, that I'd been put on this earth to be her skivvy. I felt the ache of that thought and the pain that went with it. I wanted to lash out, to make her feel like she made me feel. But I didn't do it outright. I found backhanded, under-handed, sly ways to get my own back on her.

My grandparents were complicit in my endeavour. They were the kind of parents that found fault in everything their daughter did. So any ammunition I could provide, they would load up and use against her. I cottoned on to this and learned how to complain about my mum to one of them, then stand aside like an innocent bystander and watch the assault take place. It made me feel like I had someone on my side. They spoke up for and defended me. They loved me best. Whatever imagined misdemeanour I told them about, they would reprimand my mum on my behalf.

I would wait until I had one of them on their own.

"Grandad, if I tell you something, you won't tell Mum, will you?" I would say, knowing full well he would. "Of course not, Maria. It'll be our secret," he would say.

As a teenager, I used more overt ways to get one over on her. I would fight and argue with her, then give her the cold shoulder for weeks on end. As an adult, I told her, time and time again, what a terrible mother she was.

God, forgive me I did that. God, forgive my innocence, and forgive my grand-parents for their complicity in the scheme.

I was in pain. A kid who suffered and was scared. So it's no surprise I would lash out at the person who looked like the cause. My mum seemed the obvious culprit.

I didn't know it was not her fault, that I was responding to my own thoughts and ideas about how she should be as a mother. I judged her and laid the blame at her feet for my insecurities and anxiety. It looked to me like, if I could hurt her, then maybe I could feel better.

So yes! I did cause her a lot of pain and my fervent wish is that this book is an apology to her.

29
CHOCOLATE, PORRIDGE AND INSIGHT

Today I'm having porridge for breakfast and I've always hated porridge. How could it taste so appetising? I threw in some blueberries, bananas, raisins, walnuts and apple and by God, it was delicious! It's not even made with proper milk!

I read this brilliant book called The End of Diabetes by Dr. Joel Fuhrman. He suggested everyone should cut out all animal protein. I mean initially, I was like, are you kidding me, because that means my beloved chocolate too.

Well, something flipped in my brain, because I don't crave chocolate like I did before. Of course, there's loads of chocolate in the fridge. It's been Christmas, for goodness' sake. But now, when I look at it, our relationship has changed.

As I have shared on these pages, I am a self-confessed chocoholic, with no desire whatsoever to give it up. Yet I've not had any chocolate for a fortnight. I will not get worked up about it, nor will I do anything so rash as to forbid myself from ever having chocolate again. But I do want to give myself the chance to be and stay healthy.

I didn't even buy the book for myself! When Ash got diagnosed as borderline diabetic, not enough to need medication, but enough to realise a diet change would be helpful, I wanted to know what a healthy diet looked like. The book is not only for diabetics. It talks about the prevention of a lot of health issues. Heart related, cancer related, blood pressure related. It describes how different foods affect your body.

You'd think it would be an effort to make such a wholesale change to my diet, but it wasn't. I removed white flour and sugar from my food. Out with animal protein, in with beans, nuts and seeds, bucketfuls of green vegetables and lots of superfoods.

I wouldn't have believed it possible, but I've had some of the nicest food ever! The flavours in the recipes are off the scale. Don't get me wrong, it had some physical effects on my body that's not polite to talk about in present company, but that soon settled down.

I can't tell you what it was about this book that made the difference. I've read loads of books about health and diet and none of them impacted me in the way Dr. Furhman's did. I can't tell you what I learned that made a difference. There wasn't anything new in the book. I already knew most of what the author said. Not in an intellectual, scientific way, but I already knew which foods were healthy and which were not.

For most of my life, I've had a fickle relationship with chocolate and cake, and other food that is mostly on the naughty list. I'd wanted to change the way I ate for a long time, but somehow, nothing made it happen. So why this time? Why now? Why this book?

Those are the questions to which I don't have an answer.

I know it's to do with the power of Thought. An insight can change everything, even if I can't tell you what the insight was. Still, it shifted my relationship with food. And as a result, I found it easy to change my diet.

I don't know or care if this will last forever, but for now, let me eat my delicious porridge.

30

THIS GOD

I had a difficult relationship with God. My parents were Catholic, so they sent me to a convent school. They expected me to pray every day, go to confession on Saturday, and church on Sunday morning.

There was a big disparity between what the priest said in church and what I experienced in life. The priest told me I should love this God, pray to this God, and believe in Him. But what had this God ever done for me? This God abandoned me, allowed me to go without, and was responsible for all the hurt in my life.

The priest told me I should supplicate myself to God, and worse, I should eat His body and drink His blood to show how much I loved Him. I mean, what was I - a cannibal? And why would I do that when God allowed so much trouble on the planet?

This God allowed torture, and didn't stop wars. He let millions go hungry, allowed millions of children to be abused. Racism.

Sexism, Rape. Murder. Who was this God that sat by and watched hate take its course?

The priest told me God would cast His judgement and condemn me to hell if I didn't confess my sins. I needed to ask for forgiveness, the priest explained. But why would I, if I didn't believe in God? "Then you must love Lucifer," the priest proclaimed. Lucifer! Who was responsible for all evil.

I saw through that ruse. This God created Lucifer so He wouldn't have to take the blame.

Well, I blamed God and found Him to be at fault. I arrested Him and brought the charge. I arranged the prosecution. I proclaimed His guilt and determined His punishment. I set the guillotine and cut Him from my life, the blade as sharp as tungsten slicing through my faith. I turned my back on God; I walked away without a second glance.

Thirty years later, one April afternoon, God did something strange.

"Holy Shamoly!" I said out loud. "God and religion are not the same thing!"

I lay stretched out on a sun lounger at the bottom of the garden. A fence on two sides made it into a warm sun trap. A plum tree, with its delicate pale pink blossoms, formed a canopy above me. A cream cotton shawl with a gold scrolled edge was wrapped around my shoulders. I held it close as if it were a shield that could keep the world at bay. It was a gift from the Brahma Kumaris spiritual retreat I'd attended the weekend before. Among the silver edged clouds I could sense my dad, my nan, my grandparents and my best friend, Steve, who'd all passed away during the previous few years. I felt like I could reach out my hand and touch them, they felt so close. A cool breeze kissed my face and a waft of almond touched a memory somewhere in the recesses of my mind. The wind rustled the leaves, the way Dad used to say my name, Ria, Ria, Ria, Ria, when he lulled me to sleep.

I was on solid ground. The birds were quiet. My heartbeat smooth and steady. My mind empty, like streets in the early hours of Christmas morning. A black spider, with whitish stripes, rested in the centre of a web high to my right, the invisible strands lit up by sunlight for nanoseconds at a time.

"God and religion are not the same thing," I said. As I spoke the words again, it was with a sense of letting go.

I'd been on the spiritual retreat for two and a half days. I talked about God and spirituality. I learned to meditate, and experienced five hours of silence. But nothing that weekend affected me the way this discernment between God and religion hit me, as I lay dozing on a recliner in the garden.

It wasn't like a train had hit me at a hundred miles an hour, nor had I received a knockout punch that landed me out for the count. No lightbulb turned on in my head. No. I was hit by peace. Silk caramel schmoozed through my veins. Thoughts were removed by the gentle swell of a millpond ripple. A sense of wonderment, calm and contentment with the whole of life slowed my breath and engaged my soul.

The insight came when I lay with the warm spring sun on my body and the smell of sweet hawthorn all around, when I took some time for myself.

There are a myriad of words that point to something some would call God. I realised God was not the deity of religion, someone I needed to worship, confess to, love or even eat! It was something within me, and it had been there the whole time. I came back to God when I came back to me.

PART VI

I STEPPED OUT OF THE CAGE

Familiarity has a bitter taste
I hadn't noticed
before I tasted freedom.

According to the Oxford English Dictionary, transmutation is 'the act or an instance of changing into another form.' What's interesting to me is that these moments of transmutation aren't always the obvious ones. In life or death situations we expect life to be turned on its head. We know the world has shifted on its axis, but some of these moments of transmutation come in such an ordinary way. It's mind blowing in the true sense of the word. This is what these stories feel like. Moments that blew away misunderstanding, replaced it with awareness, and changed my world.

I stepped out of the cage and began to fly.

31

LET GO AND LET GOD

It would turn out to be the worst food poisoning I've had in my entire life. I woke up in the middle of the night, jumped out of bed and ran to the bathroom. Not quite in time.

Vomit spewed out of me before I reached the toilet. The floor was covered and I had to kneel in it. I had no time to think about that. It kept on coming. It was relentless

It got worse. I jumped up so I could sit on the toilet and retch into the sink at the same time. It kind of worked.

The content of my insides spewed out from both ends. Every last ounce of the contents of my stomach was now in the sink. Every last gram of waste from my bowels had been expunged and was now in the bowl. My innards felt like they'd been turned inside out and every last vestige cleared out.

When the vomiting and diarrhoea stopped, I couldn't stand up. I leaned forward and my head fell into my hands. I was looking down at my feet as tears rolled down and dripped onto the floor.

"Are you alright in there?" Ash called from the bedroom.

Ash and I work together, as well as being husband and wife. We were in a corporate hotel room in Uganda. Once shiny, now vomit speckled, white tiles lined the floor and walls. Soft white towels hung on the polished chrome towel rail, as yet untouched. I was naked, my head in my hands. My fleshy arms almost too weak to bear its weight.

There was vomit in my hair. Excrement soiled my legs and feet. A layer of vomit and excrement lay all around the base of the toilet. A travel size tube of toothpaste lay beside the waste paper bin, screwed up and tossed aside after every last ounce had been wrung out of it. Much like my stomach.

It was day one with the Ugandan leadership team in the morning. I told myself I'd be alright by then. The drumbeat in my head, compounded by the sharp florescent light, should have told me otherwise.

"Yes, fine," I said.

I grabbed some toilet paper and started to clean up. I rinsed the sink and used one of the pristine towels to clean up the mess. It felt criminal, but what else could I do? I couldn't leave it for the maid to find.

I had almost finished cleaning when it started again. This time I was quicker. The floor survived the onslaught.

After what seemed like forever, I got back into bed. "Don't worry, Ash," I said. "I'll be better by morning. I'll be okay to be with the team." Wishful thinking, again.

Five minutes later, I was in the bathroom again.

It went on all night. I'd think my stomach and bowels were empty. Then it would start all over again.

By the early hours of the morning, I'd given up hope of being ready to work with the team at nine o'clock. But I was still deluding myself. "Perhaps I'll join you mid-morning," I said.

"Okay," Ash said. I later found out he was humouring me.

At eight thirty, Ash went off to work and soon after, the maid arrived. I was mortified. No one should have to clean that mess up. "I'm sorry," I said.

She asked if I was sick. I could barely answer. I buckled under her kind eyes. When I nodded, she said "Would you like me to get the doctor? We have one in the hotel."

When Ash returned mid-morning to check on me, I'd already spoken to the doctor and a nurse was with me. She'd brought a drip, and she was trying to get the needle into a vein on the back of my hand. My veins were non-existent. Every ounce of fluid had been drained from my body. Three times she tried without success. "I need to get a smaller needle," she said, and off she went to find one.

"Don't worry, Ash," I said. "I'll be fine by this afternoon. Maybe I'll join you for the last hour of the day."

It seems ridiculous now as I write this story, that I thought I was going to be well enough to work that day, that I would make a miraculous recovery. Ridiculous to think I had any control over it.

The nurse returned with another needle. She took it out of its wrapping and picked up my hand, ready to push it into my vein.

"God help me," she said. I was lying in the bed, wrapped up in crisp sheets. She looked like an angel in white, hovering at my side. The room seemed light and bright, even though the black-out curtains were pulled closed. Her soft, dark hand held my pale one. An amethyst glinted in the ring on her finger. “He will,” I said.

As I spoke, I heard the words, ‘Let go and let God.’ They reverberated in my mind, like an echo bouncing between mountains, and then, absolute silence.

A peace flowed through me like I’d never known before. The noise in my mind vanished. A quiet stillness of profound depth washed through me. I felt every muscle in my body relax and let go. The peaceful feeling started in my heart and expanded out in every direction. It filled every atom of my body. The feeling was absolute bliss. It felt like a sheet of the purest, softest, silk caressed my whole body. I have no other words to describe it. Words do not do it justice.

The needle went in the first time. The nurse got me hooked up to the saline solution and told me she’d check on me later in the day and the doctor would phone me.

Ash had to get back to the team. “Tell them I’ll see them later,” I told him. “Okay,” he said. “You just rest.”

I lay on the bed with the drip in my arm. The pole stood guard. The solution dripped into my listless body.

The entire night I’d been fighting the poison in my body. Determined it wouldn’t get the better of me. I thought I could beat it with the sheer force of my will. I would make myself better so I could get back to work.

‘Let go and let God.’

With those words, the fight stopped. I surrendered. It wasn’t a conscious thing.

I’d been trying to exert the full force of my will power over something that was not within my control. I couldn’t heal my body or rid it of the poison and rejuvenate it. My body would do that. The intelligence of life would do that. I found myself at peace with what was happening in my body. I knew it would sort itself out, without my input and in its own good time.

I recognised I do that with many other aspects of my life. I try to exert control over things which I have no control. The second I stopped, the intelligence of life did what it does. It healed my body.

I didn't get to see the team that day, but I managed the following day. One of them asked me whether I regretted being so ill.

"I would go through it all again so I could experience the insight," I replied. "That insight has changed my life."

The insight? The intelligence of life has got it covered. I am not in control.

32

A LITTLE THING LIKE DEATH

I took my dad for granted. I thought he'd be here forever. And then one day, without so much as a 'by your leave,' he was gone. No warning. No goodbye. No time for me to say 'Thanks for everything.'

I'd never see him again. Never laugh with him. Never play with him. Never talk to him. He'd never nosy through my cupboards again. Never draw a gun on me! Never take his hat off to me. Never give me one of his rib-crushing bear hugs. Never catch me when I fell.

Everyone knew my dad as the cowboy. He fancied himself as John Wayne in one of those spaghetti westerns. No one saw him without his beloved leather cowboy hat. Not even God. Every Sunday in church, his pride and joy would sit on the wooden pew next to him while he prayed. Every Friday and Saturday night he would don his holster, complete with two reproduction guns, put on his embroidered boots and gold spurs, and with a big grin plastered all over his face, he'd rodeo off to the closest country and western dance.

He never took life too seriously, so he would not take death seriously, either. In the Chapel of Rest, he mucked about as much as ever. He lay in his coffin in his whistle and flute and played with me. He flickered with the lights. He switched them off and plunged the room into pitch darkness. I swear I heard his titter a second before they came back on. He swung the door on its hinges. It rocked back and forth before someone came crashing through. I couldn't help but laugh. He would not let me get all serious, not about a little thing like death.

He must have seen some tough stuff in his life. He'd been in the army and lost many friends. He didn't talk about it, but sometimes, like on Remembrance Sunday, when he'd sit and watch the televised ceremony from Westminster, he'd have tears in his eyes. He wouldn't move until his military comrades had completed their march past and saluted the thousands who lost their lives through war. Then he'd stand up, shake it off and then he'd be the cowboy he always was.

My dad was strong as an ox, which is why it was so unexpected. The doctor told us he couldn't get the needle in his arm because his skin was as tough as the leather of his hat. Thick skinned, both physically and emotionally. They couldn't understand how he remained conscious, when the pain must have been off the scale. I wonder if that was the story of his life? Bear the pain and don't let his loved one's see it.

All that aside, he was the happiest man I knew. He was grateful for what he had and didn't pay attention to what he didn't. He enjoyed life fully. He taught me about that, but I didn't learn the lesson until much later.

It's only in recent years I live my life in the way he taught me. Live in joy. I'm sorry, Dad, I didn't get the lesson sooner. I didn't appreciate that about you when you were here. I'm sorry I did all the rubbish stuff to mum, because I didn't pay attention to your lessons. Thanks for not rubbing it in, and for not forcing it down my throat. You showed me the way and let me find it out for myself.

33

NEAR DEATH EXPERIENCE

I look at the steel pen in my hand. It has a British Airways logo on the side and a reassuring weight. I love it, although in theory, I shouldn't. It should be a reminder of the day my husband nearly died.

I remember Ash staggering in the aisle of the plane. Instinct told me this time he wasn't messing about.

"Ash!" I cried out.

We were on a British Airways airbus, twenty minutes into an eight-hour flight to London. We'd been working with leadership teams in Nairobi and Johannesburg.

Both of us stood in the aisle between regimented rows of slate grey seats, filled with passengers hunkering down for the night. Some nestled under blankets. Others tried to alleviate the onset of boredom by watching one of the blockbuster films available. None suspected the drama that was about to unfold.

The cabin had been sprayed with insecticide and the acrid smell scraped my tonsils, despite the peppermint sweet I'd popped into my mouth. The window shutters were closed, and the lights had been dimmed. The thrum of the engines made my shout seem like a whisper.

Ash's black sleep mask was perched on his forehead like a peak. His salt and pepper hair stuck out at angles under the elastic, and made him look like some mad professor. Bose headphones were draped around his neck. He'd been all set to sleep when he'd felt nauseous. Ash stood up to use the restroom, and now he looked like a man lost in a labyrinth.

Beads of sweat had formed on his brow. The skin of his face had taken on a translucent quality. He appeared to be looking in my direction, but his eyes were like glass.

"Oh my God, Ash!" I said, as his legs buckled beneath him and he fell towards me. For a second, I felt his dead weight, until two quick-witted, burly but agile guys came to my rescue before Ash could crush me.

This pen should, by rights, take me back to that crippling, debilitating, gut wrenching fear. It should remind me of the helplessness and impotence I experienced as I watched the unperturbed composure of the cabin crew and their hours of training kicking in. They took control with reassuring calm, did their stuff, and saved Ash's life.

When Ash was settled with an oxygen mask over his nose and mouth, asleep in the cocooned luxury of a private bed and I, in my complimentary, fine knit pyjamas, snuggled under a duck down duvet, the cabin crew laughed and made light of the part they'd played, as if it were a normal day at the office. They gave me a Liberty, paisley print, treat-filled pouch as if I was an everyday, first-class passenger. In the pouch I found this pen.

Don't ask me why I didn't throw it away, along with the other goodies in the pouch. I should want no part of the memory. But the memory just sits there, as all painful memories should. It rests in the quiet of my mind. It shows up every so often, like a nightmare in daytime slumber, or in an idle interval. It shows up like a ghostly apparition when it's least expected, a wispy cloud in a clear blue sky. Then it leaves, a puff of steam that dissipates as a new thought takes its place and relegates that painful memory to one of the shelves in the library of my mind.

34

FUCK!

I never swear. In fact, I have a reputation for not swearing. Swear words don't occur to me very often, and when they do, I censor myself. Even if I decide to say the word, it doesn't come out with its full force. It's whispered. Or half said. Or shortened. Or spluttered into a cup of tea. Especially the F word. See - I can't even write it.

The censorship is too strong. The word is in my head, but I can't write it. I can write HELL! DAMN is okay, too. Even SHIT. But F! - What's wrong with me?

I don't mind when other people use the word. But me - I'm not allowed.

Today, I will not stop until the word is written on the page in its full glory. I know that. But look what happens.

My hand doesn't move. I feel the pen's weight in my fingers and the vast emptiness of the blank line.

I say the word in my head. It doesn't feel so bad.

So let's get it down, loud and proud on the page.

OKAY. Here goes nothing.

FUCK!

Ha! I did it! Exclamation mark and underlined to boot!

"FUCK!" I said it out loud.

I'm sitting on my pristine cream couch, in a prim and tidy lounge. Crisp white walls. Smooth wooden floor. I'm positioned so the bright sun can shine on me through the window and keep me lit up. It creates a halo effect on the wall behind my head. The diamond on my finger sparkles in the sun. I'd bought it with a small inheritance from my Grandma. What would she make of what I'd just written? She'd laugh that girlish giggle of hers. She had such a naughty sense of humour.

My hummingbird journal is on my lap and my silver and gold Cross pen, a gift for my 50th birthday, is in my hand. My fingernail tips look like they've been French manicured, but they're natural.

I write first thing in the morning, but it's not often this stressful. I'm still stunned by the word on the page.

I feel like St George must have felt after he'd slayed the dragon. I've beaten my censor. It's brought on a hot flush. But I'm okay. I survived. God didn't strike me down. I think She's having a right old laugh, as She watches me battle with myself about a single word. One that is now on the page for posterity.

"FUCK!" I said again. Proud of myself.

35
THE UPS AND DOWNS OF A HUMAN HOUR

It had been one of those days. I was out for coffee with Lorraine. We've been friends for fifteen years and have been through our share of ups and downs. My latte and her Americano sat on the table between us, along with the leftover crumbs from a large piece of lemon drizzle cake we'd shared.

"How's business?" Lorraine asked.

We were sitting outside Costa Coffee at the edge of a pedestrian walkway. It was early spring and, whilst it was sunny, it wasn't warm enough to go without a coat. Mine was a long blue puffer style wrapped under my bottom to shield me from the cold wicker seat. Lorraine sported a purple ensemble with an orange coloured thick woollen scarf. It reminded me of the poem 'Warning' about a woman who is going to wear purple with a red hat when she is old. Except Lorraine isn't old. She has a fresh complexion and bright eyes that belie her fifty years.

"Everything's great," I said. "But if you'd have asked me an hour ago, it would have been a whole other story."

I'd had a recent meeting with a project manager for a large company, who was looking for an executive coach. I'd convinced myself he'd pick me. I knew I could help him and all the signs were encouraging. Some things I'd said had resonated with him and I'd observed a change in him when he had an insight.

So it was a shock when I received his email saying he'd chosen the other coach. He was very kind. Said he'd gained a lot from the conversation, but his instinct told him to opt for the other person. Bloody instinct!

I felt like a bullet train had hit me. The wind knocked right out of my sails and I had to fight for breath. When my sister, Zoe, was seven, she fell twenty feet from a tree and had been winded. Now I knew how she'd felt.

I had thought I was done with this reaction to rejection, but this time it had brought a bunch of old feelings back with a vengeance.

I'd watched my thinking and my reactions to it. It started with a load of questions. What had I done wrong? What did I say wrong? What had I missed? What's wrong with me?

They weren't questions; they were accusations. The allegation was that I'd done or said something wrong, that I'd missed something obvious, that I was piss poor at my job. The questions were daggers that pierced my skin from the inside out.

The thinking spiralled ever downwards. Who do I think I am to do this job? Who would want to engage me, anyway? I'm useless. I'm a failure. My life's a failure. My business is a failure. I'll never work again. I might as well give up the ghost, throw in the towel, jack it all in.

Failure was a seething volcano waiting to erupt. The end of the world was nigh.

I'm not a stranger to rejection. It's a well-worn path even though a less trudged one of late. Which was why the strength of the hurt feelings came as such a big surprise. I'd imagined the emery board of life had smoothed the rough edges of rejection. But there I was, flinching inside, smarting from the shock, cowering in a corner, still cradling my weakened heart.

The difference these days is that I know what's happening. I don't believe the thoughts and I'm not caught by the emotions, however strongly they pull. I know not to act from them.

So I hadn't replied to the project manager yet. I knew better than that. I'd put it to one side and invited Lorraine for a coffee instead.

36
POND SCUM AND BUTTERFLIES

There's a line in the film My Best Friend's Wedding; *I'm the pus that infects the mucus, that cruds up the fungus, that feeds on the pond scum.'* That summed up how it felt to be me.

Everyone was better than me. No matter how successful I looked from the outside, on the inside, it was still true.

Fear dominated my thinking. I was riddled with anxiety. Full of self-judgement and self-criticism. I was in a constant battle with my own ineptitude. As far as I was concerned, I was a disaster area, a letdown, a complete and utter failure.

I had become a self-development addict. I would take every opportunity to try to better myself. I wanted to improve and, whilst I was at it, prove to the world I was something I wasn't. It was like trying to metamorphose every cell in my body, one by one, when it wasn't I who had the power to change them.

So here I was, on a Saturday morning in July, in a village hall in Essex, with my husband, ready to listen to some guy from America. Part of me wondered if he would be the one to teach me the strategy that would make me feel better. I didn't hold out much hope.

We were congregated in rows with seventy other people. There was a small stage at the front of the hall, with deep burgundy velvet curtains hiding the paraphernalia I guessed was backstage. It smelled the same as every other village hall across the UK - damp and mouldy. Flecks of dust dangled in the air, caught in a streak of sunlight that came through the window near the ceiling. We were seated on chairs as hard as concrete, in the back row, ready to make a quick exit if need be. The man from America bobbed about on stage between the sea of heads in front of us. His name was Dr. Dicken Bettinger. What kind of a name is that?

He talked about a flower he'd watched grow up the side wall of his house. I wasn't paying much attention.

"When the vine reached a window or an obstacle," he said, "it turned a right angle."

I sat hunched over, with my legs crossed, a thick wool shawl tucked under my calves. I was absorbed by the Birkenstock that hung from my foot and the candy pink toenails that contrasted with the cream leather of the shoe. At the edge of my sight was a dirty glob of chewing gum that was so ingrained, it looked like part of the wooden floorboard.

"How does it do that?" Dicken said.

Something shifted in my chest, like the click of a combination lock on one of those old bank vaults. The solid steel door swung open, and a casing around my heart shattered. I broke free of old heavy chains. I emerged like a butterfly from a chrysalis. I had no idea what had happened.

It was an insight. A serious, life-changing, aha moment. A mind-altering eureka. An instantaneous shift. It was a falling back into who I am at my core. A transformation, even though I didn't recognise it as such. It's only when I look back I feel the magnitude of what happened.

I had no clue that everything had changed. My former life became like a reflection in a glass window - a hint of something that isn't really there. A radical shift happened inside of me, while my outer world stayed the same. My inner world changed into one of peace, faith, hope and optimism, my mind fuelled by joy and happiness.

I am no longer pond scum, nor do I need to change myself, cell by cell. I no longer battle with constant fear. I am not the lowest of the low. I know who I really am.

37

I STEP OUT OF THE CAGE

Nothing happened today. Well, nothing visible to the naked eye. Yet it will shape the rest of my life.

I was at Dicken's house in La Conner, Washington, on the coast of the Pacific Ocean. Dicken Bettinger, my friend and mentor.

"Nothing on the inside can hurt you," he said. Autumn sunshine streamed into the room. Thirteen other people dissipated like a mirage in the desert and I was left alone on an upright padded recliner in this warm and cosy lounge. Hummingbirds were frozen in mid-flight on the sugary feeder hanging outside the large patio window.

My body became one with the cosmos. I melted into the spaciousness, the vastness, the universal all-ness words cannot explain. My eyes were closed, yet more open than ever. I was aware of nothing and everything, all at the same time. My heart brimmed with something far greater than the word 'love' can describe, but love is the only word that comes close.

Dicken's voice hummed in the background.

"My thoughts can't hurt me," I said to myself.

My eyes, fuelled by emotion, had overflowed with healing waters. I welcomed the tears that ran smooth and unchecked down my cheeks.

As they left my body, something else left with them. Something toxic, dark and sinister that had inhabited, inhibited, and distorted my life. Something I'd carried with me for as long as I can remember.

I felt purified and energised. Drained, empty, and sated, all at the same time. I was alive in a way I never had been before. Freedom had come into view, no longer hidden beyond a horizon. Spaciousness revealed itself in my chest, where a rock had lodged itself many years before. A breath, a blessed relief, had been sighed.

A holding on, let go.

A door opened.

I stepped out of the cage.

PART VII

HOW I ACCLIMATIZED TO THE OUTSIDE WORLD

I trust the intelligence behind life,
peace reigns.
I forget and it's chaos.

Once I'd broken free of the cage I had to see what life could really be like. Life was so different, it took a bit of getting used to.

When I broke free, it didn't stop me from experiencing life's trials, but my navigation of the vagaries of life has changed.

I am able to traverse life's fluctuations differently. I run into old habits of thinking and move through them in a more fluid way. I observe what goes on in my mind, which gives me clarity and an easier, more graceful experience of life.

Here are some examples of what it was like getting used to being outside the cage.

38

I CHANGED MY MIND

I was a timid, shy person,
scared of my own shadow,
hiding myself away, hoping not to be seen.

I was scared people would see
the real me, reject me
because I wasn't worth
the time of anyone's day.

I hid the meanest part of me,
the jealous, resentful, cruel part of me.

I hid the hate.

I hated the goodness of others.
Their wealth, their happiness,
everything they had that I didn't.

I hated what that meant
about me.

I pretended
I didn't need anything,
friends, company.
I didn't need birthday parties
or sleepovers.

I didn't need love.

I built a wall around me.
One that kept everyone out,
and my feelings in
where they festered,
and infected my reality.

One day, my mind changed.

I saw how my reality was shaped,
how Thought created my experience,
how I was full of light
and darkness was an illusion.
I saw endless possibility.

It changed everything.

It dismantled the wall in a nanosecond.
Loosened the grip of fear-fuelled thoughts.
Released toxic energy into the ether
where it dissipated and disappeared.

No harm done.

Now I am free as an eagle that soars
on a warm draft of air.
I am off the hook of my own hangman's noose.

I changed my mind.

And when I did,
my experience of life changed,
my worldview changed.
My life changed.

39

MIND ON THE STEERING WHEEL

I have an innate wisdom that guides me and has done so even in my darkest times. I sometimes refer to it as the intelligence behind life. Sydney Banks called it Mind. I like to think of it as the steering wheel in my human experiences.

I notice in life and death scenarios I yield to something greater than myself. It's like I have no choice, no control whatsoever, so I'm quick to give up the fight, surrender to what will be and await the ultimate outcome. Not so in more ordinary situations.

Like when our visas and passports got held up at the post office a few days before we were due to travel. Like when the train was delayed, and I thought I'd be late. Like when I lost my glasses and, after hours of looking, resigned myself to buying a new pair, then later found them in the fridge. Where else would they have been!

I'm not so quick to see this intelligence during those times. Times when something gets thrown in from left of field, unexpected, outside the bounds of my well constructed, designed to be stress-free plans. They send me into a tailspin.

Like the time I wrote a blog about writing this book. I mentioned that I'd asked people to read what I'd written and give me feedback; to see if they understood what I was pointing towards, what I was sharing.

Within hours, I received an email from an academic in Canada. He was a master coach, and a relative stranger, and he offered to take part in my feedback process.

Oh my God, did I fall into a tailspin! Fear raised its ugly head and threw me into turmoil. A tsunami of thought captured and paralysed me. In my mind, he would damn my book all the way to hell and back.

I'd already gathered my little band of merry volunteers, so my knee jerk reaction was to send a 'Thanks but no thanks' message to his inbox. But I needed a reasonable excuse, any reason I could fathom, to refuse his request. I wanted to curl up into a tiny ball and hide myself from his inevitable scorn. So I didn't reply.

The next day, a new thought popped into my mind.

"What if this is the Intelligence of Life?" I said to Ash.

He stood next to me in the kitchen. I waited for the kettle to boil. The dried tea leaves were in the pot ready for the hot water. Ash had mowed the lawn that morning, and the smell of fresh cut grass came through the open window.

"What are you talking about?" he asked.

Having a complete stranger review the book was not part of my well-defined plan. But what if this outsider had been sent by the Intelligence of Life?

Perhaps this person, four thousand miles away, would offer an alternative; a contrary, objective view of my book? I mean, isn't that what I wanted? Maybe the Intelligence of Life wanted to open my eyes to the reality of what would happen when my book was published.

"What if this man from Canada is the Intelligence of Life with its hand on the steering wheel?" I said.

I saw how previous, so-called 'curses' had turned into blessings in my life, although I hadn't seen it at the time. I saw how every calamity had been a life lesson when I looked back on it with the benefit of hindsight. Every time things had veered off the route of my meticulous plan, I'd learned something new.

When I saw this, I surrendered. The storm in my mind settled to a gentle breeze. The foghorn of my ego fell silent. I stopped trying to second guess life. I love how when I stop doing that, an answer presents itself, like when I found my glasses in the fridge! Later that day, I wrote to Michael, the master coach from Canada, to thank him for his kind offer and, with not an ounce of anxiety (more like a kilo!) I sent a few chapters for him to read.

40
THE PARADOX THAT IS FEAR

I'd finished a talk about coaching presence at a conference in London. As I walked off the stage, a woman with a short blonde bob, in a pristine trouser suit, and white silk blouse, headed towards me. She reminded me of me a long time ago. I noticed a copy of my book in her hand. We came together at the bottom step. I thought the talk had gone well, but you never know with this topic. It's not rocket science, just good old common sense, but not many people talk about it the way I do. Most favoured the academic or neuro-scientific approach to coaching. I'd seen a few heads nod in agreement while I talked, but I wasn't sure if hers was one of them. She looked like she could be an academic.

"Could I ask you something?" she said.

The conference room hummed with the noise of people shuffling and stretching their limbs after an hour of sitting in one position. I can be unsettled when people ask first, if they can ask a question, sometimes it means they have a contrary point to make.

I stood in front of her in a soft pearly wool frock, a cerise scarf draped around my neck. It had one-inch tassels all along the edge. My long, strawberry blond hair hung loose around my shoulders. She stood six inches taller than me. At one time her height would have made me feel small, but not anymore. Her heavy musk perfume was like a mist that emanated from her.

"Would you sign a copy of your book for me, please?" she asked. It wasn't what I'd expected. Whenever I do a talk about presence, I expect someone to come along and tell me what a load of codswallop it is. Science backs up what I say, but only if you read it in a certain way. I wondered if she was going to be the one to pick a fight with me. Instead, she told me how much my book had helped her. In fact, the book, and my being the speaker, was the reason she'd bought her ticket.

My mind went back to how scared I was when I wrote the book. Fear was a thread that wove itself through the process from beginning to end. I was afraid when I handed the first chapter to someone to read, afraid when I invited feedback from a group of critical friends. I feared they would find it boring, that everyone would criticise and find fault with it. I was afraid it wouldn't get published, and I was even more afraid that if it did, it would be a colossal flop.

My heart was in my mouth when I handed in the final manuscript to the publisher. What if the editor thought it was a pile of crap, despite what my friends had said? Who was I to publish a book, anyway? Was I about to wreck my career and my reputation?

If I was so scared, how come the book got published? That's a question I have pondered. As well as the fear, there was something that pushed me from the inside. It kept me going. It kept me writing and editing, kept me getting up in the early hours of the morning to write for up to fourteen hours a day. I'd wake early, get up and go sit at the kitchen table. I would go from my bed to my laptop and write. And write. And write.

I never considered what the process might be for writing a book. I assumed I would write it and - hey presto - it would be fully formed. Once I'd completed a few chapters it was obvious it was a brain dump. Terry Pratchett says the first draft is just the story making itself known to the author. Once that was written, I had to create a structure, which then needed repeated edits, refinement and clarification. Hours, days and weeks of it.

If it were any other task, I would have thought of it as a slog. But this, I loved. It's a paradox. I hated the fear, but I loved what I was doing, the whole process. All ten chapters. All the versions. All fifteen rewrites.

I tell you something. If I'd have appreciated what it would take to publish a book, I wouldn't have agreed to a six-month deadline, but I did. When I handed in the manuscript, just two weeks late, the publisher was surprised it was done. She thought I'd ask for an extension.

No one told me it was an almost impossible bar to reach, so I did it anyway. And the rest, as they say, is history. The book was translated into Russian and South Korean and has been read in twenty-two countries.

Something pushed me, drove and guided me to write that first book, in spite of my fearful thinking. That same something operates in other parts of my life. Times when I've been scared, anxious, worried, and yet something keeps me going. It tells me I'm doing the right thing, and it says do it regardless of what I'm thinking. I know not to question it; it never lets me down.

41
THE WITCHING HOUR

A menopausal night sweat had kept me awake. Again. This was the third night on the trot without sleep. I was so dog-tired I could cry.

My mind felt like someone had injected it with a hallucinogenic drug. Thoughts spun in my head, like a churlish, freaking carousel. I bashed and plumped the pillow as if it was to blame. I kept turning it to find a sweet cold spot, but that eluded me, too.

"What's happening?" Ash asked, half asleep.

He was burrowed under a kingsize pile of luxury, ivory Egyptian cotton. I'd kicked my half of the duvet off me and onto him. A sliver of moonlight shone through the tiny gap in the blackout curtains. A hint of Olbas oil lingered on the smooth pillow. On top of a small pine bedside cabinet, level with my eyes, was the green neon of an LED clock. It was 3:00am.

A navy scrunchy on the pillow had escaped my long hair. I'd tied it up in an effort to stay cool. I was naked except for a pair of bright mauve and yellow bed socks. My feet were like blocks of ice despite the heat that raged in the rest of my body.

"Nothing," I said. "I'm going downstairs. You go to sleep."

I'd tried to read, to create a distraction from the magic roundabout of thoughts. Nothing stopped the protracted repetitive conversations that took place with non-existent people in my head.

They're one sided. A unique monologue because my impoverished mind can't fabricate the other person's contribution to the exchange.

I'd not noticed before that the fanciful dialogues I have in my mind are only ever one side of the supposed discourse, nor how parrot-like these phantasmal scenarios are. I say one thing and it boomerangs back to me, echoes to and fro in my mind. The problem with imaginary conversations is that there's nothing to respond to, nothing to bounce off, so the story has nowhere to go.

You'd think that would put me to sleep, put me out of my excruciating misery, but it doesn't. Instead, my mind moves on to the next non-existent, mythical talkfest.

That's how I ended up writing at this godforsaken hour of the morning, in the vain hope I can sidetrack the bustle in my mind and trick it into inertia. I pray I will exhaust the diatribe and get back to sleep.

I try not to struggle against the thoughts, and to let them have their way. I know they will pass of their own accord. I want the race in my head to reach the finish line, but there are a lot of runners in this mental marathon.

The struggle is not the conversation, or the content of my thinking, but the battle to gain control. The wish for it all to go away, for it all to stop. The longing for something other than what is happening right now.

There's a deeper part of me who doesn't struggle, who observes the wrestling match and knows there is nothing to fight with, nothing to battle, and nothing to rail against. That part of me knows the only thing I grapple with is myself, that the thoughts will wear themselves out and when they do, I will fall asleep.

42

A FISH OUT OF WATER

I was at a high-class business dinner last night and I felt like a fish out of water. Fifty invited guests milled around the Jacobean ballroom of a boutique hotel, the former home of an immensely wealthy family. I stood next to a tall round table with my friend Janet and another woman I'd only just met. They chatted away like they'd known each other forever. I was opposite the huge leaded window, blinded by the evening sun that was low in the sky. I couldn't move away because I was hemmed in by one of a dozen large sofas dotted around. Beautiful, bold fabrics adorned the windows, and a family crest loomed above a five-hundred-year-old stone fireplace that would have eclipsed my entire house.

Magnums of champagne and gleaming cut glasses rested on polished antique bureaus and tables. Waitresses in black dresses and little white aprons discreetly topped up glasses that were still half full. Waiters, in uniform trousers and shirts, carried trays of canapés, miniature portions of steak and chips, teeny versions of roast beef and Yorkshire pudding, quails' eggs and smoked salmon on coin-sized blinis. I couldn't decide whether to pop them into my mouth whole or nibble them whilst holding my little finger in the air.

I had a crystal flute in my hand, an over-confident smile pasted on my face and a head full of thoughts: I'm not rich enough, not pretty enough, not clever enough, not trendy enough, and not young enough to mix with this echelon of people. I didn't drive the right car, live in a big enough home, or have the right amount of money in my bank account. I was a square peg in a round hole, a second-rate Annie, an extra jigsaw piece in the wrong box.

"Maria, this is Sandra," Janet said. "Sandra sold her company a little while ago and now she keeps herself busy running a small recruitment business."

Janet was a vision in coral. She headed up a family business that would give any of the FTSE 100 companies a run for their money. It was a constant surprise to me that we'd come to be friends and that she'd invited me as her guest to this prestigious event. Her outfit was from Harvey Nichols, her matching shoes, adorned with a large buckle, were Jimmy Choo. Sandra was dressed in a swirling green shift dress with a matching cardigan with voile panels at the front. It was subtle and expensive. I was embarrassed by my high street brand flowered skirt and top, and peep-toe wedged shoes. The lot had cost me a week's salary, and still it didn't cut the mustard. A dog treat sat on the Persian carpet by an enormous writing desk. I figured one of the staff would be in for the high jump if anyone spotted it there. The champagne bubbles had left a piquant zing in my mouth.

"How lovely to meet you," I said as Janet and Sandra picked up the conversation where they'd left off. It was clear I was to be included in it, but as they continued to talk about their respective businesses, I had half an ear to other conversations going on. I caught a snippet between two dapperly attired men to one side of me.

"So what car did you go for in the end?" the taller of the two said. "Of course I went for the Land Rover Discovery," the other said. His voice was two decibels higher than it needed to be. "There's a question mark about their reliability, but it does make a statement. Don't you agree?"

Sandra looked at me and I noticed the dark turquoise eyeshadow on her lower eyelid; it seemed a little incongruous with the quiet smile and neatly bobbed hair. I looked at Janet, who sported a dash of bright pink lipstick. Earlier she'd said she felt like she needed a splash of colour. I, too, wore make-up, which for me was most unusual. I wondered what required us to paint on a face before we set foot in this place.

As I looked around, I was struck, not by the expensive cars or the million pound loans they talked about, nor the designer clothes, nor by how much money must have existed in that room alone, if you added it all up. What caught my attention was the humanity. The little clues that showed people's anxieties, the desire to make a good impression, the need to please others and the endeavour to have a pleasant time despite their nervousness. All the things that went through my mind, too.

I saw the person behind the mask of overt confidence, the talk of large houses, lavish holidays and huge business successes. I saw we all had our insecurities and our human frailties and I saw I fitted right in, because, at the end of the day, on the inside we are all the same.

43

SLOTH - THE SEVENTH DEADLY SIN

I'm groggy this morning. The jet lag has got me. I was so tired yesterday, I went to bed shit crazy early. I thought that would do it. Maybe I'd wake up in the morning and feel on top of the world.

Now my head feels like someone's poured molasses into my brain. It feels like my limbs are filled with wet concrete. My hand is tempted to write the word 'sloth.'

In the past, I would've tried to fight the tiredness. Tried to force my body to move. I'd attempt to trick my mind into action, jimmy the molasses out of my head.

Last night after we arrived home, I told Ash, "For once I'd like to take a whole day off to sit and read." I hadn't done that in so long.

"Why don't you?" he asked.

We were in the lounge. Ash standing on the red rug in front of the ebony-tiled hearth. Bronze hares sat with their ears pricked up waiting for my response. My first thought was indignant. I can't do that. I don't have time to waste a day reading. I'm far too busy. But another followed it, a more tentative thought. What if I could? Was this a luxury I could afford?

Something stirred in my heart.

"I might just do that," I said.

It sounded shit crazy to me. Me, who thought being a lazy-bones the worst of the seven deadly sins. I thought I should be busy all the time.

That had all made perfect sense to me. Before.

Before I recognised that life lives me, not the other way around.

PART VIII

HOW I SETTLED INTO FREEDOM

I know not to believe my thinking,
unless
it wishes me well.

The best thing about my learning so far was remembering who I am underneath and beyond all of my thinking, the coming back to my own spiritual essence: that I am a spiritual being having a human existence. I am free, and always have been. Only my thinking denied me that freedom.

Knowing who I really am was the crowning glory. This gave me freedom from the caged life I was living.

44

I ALWAYS WANTED TO BE ENLIGHTENED

PART I

I want what Eckhart Tolle has.
What Sydney Banks had.
What the Dalai Lama has.
And I want it now.

Enlightenment must be better
than this roller coaster, spinning wheel
of an angst-ridden life.

I want peace.
I want to feel okay.
I want to be happy.

I want to be confident and self-assured.
I want to be calm and collected.
I want to be thoughtful and wise.

I never want to feel angry or anxious,
jealous or resentful,
guilty or ashamed.

I want life on an even keel,
a millpond existence,
no mountains to climb,
no depths to fall into.

If I were enlightened,
I wouldn't have to experience
all the ups and downs
of life's traumas.
I wouldn't have to suffer.

PART II

But this wanting
is, in effect,
a desire not to be human.

Being human is to experience all of life's emotions.
Enlightenment doesn't remove life's dramas.
I don't need to be different to feel okay.

Who I am is always okay.
Who I am can always cope with trauma.
Who I am is designed to experience
all that life throws at me
and all that life has to offer.

Being human gives me the opportunity
to experience everything,

every single facet,
every single nuance,
every single colour of life's great tapestry.

Being human would be pretty boring,
if I'd been granted my version
of enlightenment.

45
INVISIBLE

Jenny is the youngest eighty-four-year-old woman I know. She is my oldest and dearest friend and last week we were out clothes shopping in Leicester, which is just an excuse for us to spend some time together.

"I feel invisible," Jenny said. We'd been talking about ageing.

We were in John Lewis's café, our regular stop for coffee and cake. We sat in red leather armchairs with jute shopping bags leaning against their legs. The bags were filled with an array of new clothes for me. Jenny hadn't bought anything. It was rare for her to buy things for herself these days.

The smooth aroma of a café latte steamed on the table in front of me. Jenny had her usual pot of tea for one. We'd shared a slice of Victoria sponge.

A group of teenage girls sat at a nearby table, laughing and swapping stuff they'd found on their phones. A young man sat at another table, his eyes glued in their direction.

"I know what you mean," I said.

I'd been out with my beautiful eighteen-year-old stepdaughter, the week before, when a young man looked in our direction. I saw the flirtation and longing in his smile. There was a time I used to be on the receiving end of such glances.

Somewhere along the line, those looks of appreciation had faded away. Somewhere along the line, I'd become an old lady. I'd become invisible.

"But I don't feel my age," I said. Jenny nodded in agreement.

I feel young on the inside. The bodywork might be a little rusty, the engine in need of a little oil and grease, the pistons may give a creak under pressure, but the energy that powers the engine is as dynamic and vigorous as ever. My body may have deteriorated, but the life force within me is no less stunning. I shine from the inside.

46
RAINING LIKE A BANSHEE

I met my sister for lunch last week, when the weather would have given Noah a run for his money.

"Has the weather been getting you down?" Dawn asked.

We were seated in St Francis' tearoom, a volunteer run café attached to the local abbey. Mismatched tables were covered with a patchwork mix of donated tablecloths, and the chairs had been reupholstered with fabric offcuts. The walls, shelved from floor to ceiling, were filled with handmade items made by local, wannabe craft people. There were pictures with quasi-inspirational quotes like 'Live Life' and 'May the sea be your oyster' stencilled onto old maps. Necklaces made of bottle tops and ring pulls hung on papier-mâché hands that reached into the air.

I wondered whether they ever sold any of the products. Perhaps they do. I imagine the people who make them and those who buy them. I guess and make judgments. To make up for my unkind assumptions, I buy an item every so often, like the tweed key ring with skew whiff seams that sat on the table with my car keys attached.

It still rained like a banshee, but the light that shone through the large window next to us made the room feel bright. The hum of chatter kept the noise of the storm at bay. The aroma from my lunch of carrot and coriander soup and peppermint tea masked the charity shop smell that permeated the café.

One quirk of this café is they serve tea in china teapots that clash with the cups and saucers. Today ours was served in an English Rose teapot and paired with two Asian patterned teacups.

Dawn was seated next to me. Her thick white hair was smoothed back from her face. Freckles dotted her alabaster skin and her gorgeous smile reached all the way to the twinkle in her eyes. She had no idea how beautiful she is.

She is the ultimate girl scout, prepared for any eventuality. She carries more stuff with her than a combat soldier on exercise, including the mini screwdriver key ring with which she'd just fixed my spectacles. The rain still tapped on the window.

"No, I've been fine," I said. "Isn't this soup lovely?"

As I sipped my soup and drank my tea, I thought about Dawn's question. It's a real testament to the misunderstanding of how life works that people believe the weather gets them down. As if the five days of heavy rain and floods would impact one's mental wellbeing. There was a time when I believed that, too. But not anymore.

47
MY KIND OF CHRISTMAS

It's two days till Christmas. I've written two lists.
What I need to do today.
What I need to buy.

There's so little time.
Everything has to be done by tomorrow.

Lots to do + so little time = pressure

Pressure equals:
There's too much to do.
I'm running out of time.
I should have done it all already.
And why didn't I?

Pressure equals:
The disaster it will be, if it doesn't get done.
The apocalyptic, catastrophic failure of epic proportions
that will be laid on my shoulders.

No wonder it's so much pressure.
Where is the pressure coming from?
The question hangs in the ether.

Thought.
The answer that bounces back.

I have the power to choose.
The power to choose to pay attention or not pay attention.
The power to choose pressure or not pressure.

Christmas with pressure
was always my experience of the holiday.

Christmas without pressure
is wonderful.
It's Christmas using the power,
of Thought,
to create the opposite of pressure.

It's the true meaning of Christmas.
Peace and Joy.

It's my kind of Christmas.

48

A NEWBORN BABY SORT OF A DAY

I never thought about how fresh a new day can be. I never quite experienced the actual fact of a brand spanking new day. I've never before woken up this awake, this alive, this fertile to the possibility that yesterday no longer exists and everything starts again, right here, right now.

Every day of my life I'd woken up with a concrete yet nebulous belief that yesterday mattered. That somehow today was connected to yesterday and all the days before it.

Every day I'd acted like there was a continuous piece of string, a taut and twisted length of cable, a chunky, indestructible chain, tied to the day I was born and binding each day to the next until the day I die.

Every day I've wandered half asleep, stumbling in a half-sluggish state and perambulating in torpid drowsiness through my life, hypnotised by the illusion that I was awake.

I've never been this alive to the idea that each morning the clock resets, the slate is wiped clean, and the past is put behind me.

Never.

Not until today.

Today is different from every one of my todays before now. Today has a freshness I've never experienced. Today is a newborn baby sort of day.

49
THIS UNDERSTANDING WILL CHANGE THE WORLD

I didn't always feel like this. Like there is a special understanding I knew but had forgotten. No matter what happens in the world, I'm going to be okay. I'm able to share what I know and it can change people's lives.

It's a simple way of looking at how the mind works, yet it changed my life for the better. When Ash and I talk about how our inner lives have shifted, it triggers insights in others, and what they see changes their lives. What people learn in two days with us could have a tremendous impact on humanity. They appreciate immediately how that could happen.

"What we've learned could change the world," Lucy said.

We were in our office-come-lounge, above an Arts centre, on the grounds of a stately home in Leicestershire. The room was cosy with armchairs and scatter cushions and violet, red and cream blankets wrapped around a few of the six people on our program. On the wall behind us was a big splash of orange, abstract art.

The day was cold outside, but the winter sun bathed us in natural light and warmth. Coasters scattered on the oak coffee table bore words like 'Love is the answer.' They were half covered by tea and coffee cups and glasses of water, all filled to various levels. A bunch of yellow daffodils in a colourful, Italian jug on the sideboard, had opened up during the two days.

Everyone was dressed in comfortable clothes, sitting on comfortable chairs enjoying a comfortable silence. We'd been sharing the way we see how our mind works. They'd all seen something that had created a positive shift within them already. Lucy had told us, for the first time in her life, she'd experienced a clear mind. The difference was written all over her face. When she arrived, she'd looked tired and drawn. Her dark hair, which had been cinched into a tight bun, now hung in soft curls around her face. Her forehead and cheeks were smooth as eggs. The stress lines she'd arrived with had disappeared and the years had dropped away. She looked ten years younger. They all did. It was a moment of pure love. They basked in the truth of the words. They relaxed into their true selves and felt the effect of this simple understanding.

My heartbeat had slowed down to the pace of life.

"Yes, this understanding is changing the world," I said.

EPILOGUE

I DIDN'T BELIEVE IN GOD

I threw God
into the not to be trusted barrel.
God laughed and said, *it is good.*

When the shit hit the fan,
I shouted at God.
And God said, *it's good.*

I demanded God do something,
when war broke out.
God sighed and said, *all is good.*

In my darkest hour,
I prayed to a God I knew did not exist.
God smiled. God knew I was good.

With the sun on my face,
I thanked God for its warmth.
God beamed. It *was* good.

I didn't believe in God,
yet all my life,
I spoke to God.

God always replied,
it is good.

ACKNOWLEDGMENTS

There are so many people who have been instrumental or influential in bringing this book into the world. I thank every person who has been with me along the way. Thank you is not a big enough phrase to contain the weight of the gratitude I feel. I sincerely hope I haven't missed anyone.

Jules Swales. In 2017, over breakfast in Seattle, you prompted me to write a creative piece. I had never thought of myself as a story teller. In 2018 I became a student of Method Writing, with you as my teacher, and I have loved studying with you ever since. You are my friend, my mentor, my writing teacher and early editor. This book would never have existed, nor would it have been as well written, without your cheerleading, wise guidance and support. Thank you.

Jacqueline Hollows. Whenever this book needed some get up and go, you were there to provide it. You inspired me every time you talked about what was happening with your book. You encouraged me by always being interested enough to ask what was happening with mine. You helped it along with your coaching support and your constant 'amazing' in response to every milestone achieved. Thank you.

Jamie Fiore-Higgins. You are a role model for any professional writer. Being able to observe your writing practice at close quarters emboldened me to treat my writing as a profession, rather than a hobby. Your encouragement and support is second to none. I may not know how tall you are, but you have a big space in my heart. Thank you.

Dicken Bettinger Ed.D. My mentor for this past nine years. I have had such amazing conversations with you over Zoom and in the comfort of your home with the hummingbirds as our additional guides. Without you I would not have the level understanding of these Three Principles. For being a wonderful friend, spiritual guide and loving presence in my life. Thank you.

Coizie Bettinger. You have been a wonderful presence in my life. Someone who lives the Principles and has been my teacher, without being my teacher. For your love, kindness and unceasing encouragement for my writing, and for being an amazing role model for how to live life. Thank you.

Jan and Chip Chipman. You may not have been directly involved with this book, but you were most certainly involved in my journey into the Three Principles, without which this book would not exist. For your living the Principles and your quiet presence and friendship in my life. Thank you.

Alexis Rhone-Fancher. I am blessed to have you as one of my editors. Not only have you given me brilliant feedback for my book, you have challenged and pushed me to open doors within myself I hadn't realised still existed. For encouraging me to embrace my freedom. Thank you.

Jane Tucker. Another blessing in my life. Your editorial feedback was thoughtful and thought provoking. Your understanding of the Three Principles was a beautiful added dimension. Thank you.

Michael Cullen. Simon Foster. Elizabeth Juffs. Anne Lewis. Kev Urwin. Many moons ago, the five of you read through a handful of chapters and gave me wise and valuable feedback as potential readers of the book. For your thoughtful answers to the questions I asked. Thank you.

Steve Pitcher. (18 Design Ltd) For doing such a brilliant job of designing the book cover. You somehow take what I ask you and convert it into something I could not have imagined and is always perfect. Thank you.

Michelle Mackie. (Dolly fine art if you want to find her on Facebook.) It gives me goosebumps to think about how your incredible image came to be the cover art for my book. That is a story in its own right. To you and Wishbone Publishing Ltd for the rights to use your artwork. Thank you.

Michael Neill. For writing and publishing the Inside Out Revolution. While I was writing my first book, Ash was reading yours. Your book brought me to the Three Principles. Thank you.

Sydney Banks. Although I never had a chance to meet the man, I will always be grateful to him for bringing the Three Principles to the world. For filling my life with more grace and ease than I could ever have imagined. Thank you.

Ashley Wood. The most amazing husband a person could wish for. For your patient listening to hours and hours worth of first drafts. For your endless encouragement to write and publish. For your unfailing belief in me as a writer, a coach and a human being. For telling me you love me several times a day. (I love you too.) And for so much more. Thank you.

ABOUT THE AUTHOR

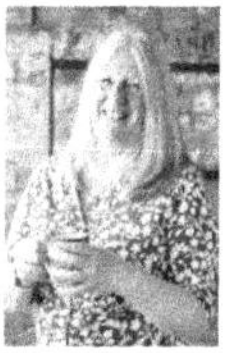

I never knew who I was and I didn't know that I didn't know.

I knew what I did. I was a business owner, a coach, a coach supervisor, a trainer, a facilitator, a mediator, an author of one book.

I knew what I was in relation to other people. A wife, a step-mum, a daughter (not a very good one, I might add), a sister, an auntie, a friend, a colleague.

I knew what I had in the material world. A successful business, a nice house and car, money in the bank, a good social life, several holidays a year.

But who I am - a spiritual essence that can never be broken - was lost under many years of habitual thinking that could be described as Imposter Syndrome, or low self-esteem, or anxiety, sometimes depression. Every day I had the constant nagging thought; I don't deserve any of this, and one day I will lose it all. I thought others didn't like me. If they were nice to me, I thought they were being kind. If anyone told me I was good at my job, I would think, one day they'll find out the truth and then where will I be?

People thought I was confident. I looked confident. I acted confident. But it was a veneer. A suit of armour I donned every day, so I could face the world.

One day my husband, Ash, introduced me to Three Principles as brought to the world by Sydney Banks, and that's when everything changed. That's what these stories are about.

I now run, not one, but two successful businesses. Meridian Iliffe Ltd and IW Press Ltd. I am still a coach, a coach supervisor etc and now I am a 3PGC registered practitioner. Plus I am a publisher and six times published author. I am still very much married to my wonderful husband.

The difference is, I have found who I am underneath all of that thinking. I have become myself. As a result I go through life with more grace and ease than I ever thought possible.

That, my dear reader, is what I want for you.

If you would like to find out more about me as a coach and how I use Three Principles in my work, have a look at www.fromquiet.co.uk

If you would like to know more about me as a publisher, author and writer's coach, check out www.iliffe-wood.co.uk

facebook.com/iliffewood
instagram.com/iliffewood
linkedin.com/in/maria-iliffe-wood-52682912
twitter.com/iliffewood

RECOMMENDED RESOURCES

If you would like to find out more about the Three Principles and/or some of the other subjects mentioned in this book - here's some of my favourites.

VIDEO AND AUDIO RECORDINGS BY SYDNEY BANKS

www.sydbanks.com

BOOKS ABOUT THREE PRINCIPLES BY SYDNEY BANKS

- The Missing Link
- The Enlightened Gardener
- The Enlightened Gardener Revisited
- Second Chance
- In Quest of the Pearl
- Dear Liza

OTHER BOOKS THAT POINT TO THE THREE PRINCIPLES

- Coming Home by Dicken Bettinger and Natasha Swerdloff
- Our True Identity… Three Principles by Elsie Spittle
- The Path to Contentment - by Elsie Spittle
- Creator by Steve Chandler
- Being Human by Amy Johnson
- The Inside-Out Revolution by Michael Neill

BOOKS THAT POINT TO THE SPIRITUAL NATURE OF OUR EXISTENCE

- The Science of Mind by Ernest Holmes
- The Power of Now by Eckhart Tolle
- Oneness with Life by Eckhart Tolle

SPIRITUAL BOOKS FOR THE SCIENTIFICALLY MINDED

- Back to Sanity by Steve Taylor
- Spiritual Science by Steve Taylor
- Infinite Potential by Lothar Schafer

OTHER RESOURCES MENTIONED IN THIS BOOK

- Method Writing with Jules Swales - www.julesswales.com
- Jack Grapes Method Writing - The First Four Concepts by Jack Grapes
- Advanced Method Writing by Jack Grapes
- The End of Diabetes by Dr Joel Fuhrman

ALSO BY MARIA ILIFFE-WOOD

WRITTEN BY MARIA

Coaching Presence: Building Consciousness and Awareness into Coaching Interventions

Daily Yarns: Riding the Lockdown Roller Coaster of Emotions

PUBLISHED AND CO-AUTHORED BY MARIA

A Different Story: How Six Authors became Better Writers

Stories from the Muses: Become a Better Writer

INCLUDES A CONTRIBUTION FROM MARIA

From the Heart: Explorations in True Nature and Unconditional Love

CPSIA information can be obtained
at www.ICGtesting.com
Printed in the USA
LVHW030504110922
728014LV00014B/440

9 781838 333058